THE GREAT WILD

SILENCE

THE GREAT WILD SILENCE

Ruminations and Excursions
in the Adirondacks

by

Walt McLaughlin

Wood Thrush Books

The cover photo of Pillsbury Lake in the morning
was taken by Walt McLaughlin

Published by Wood Thrush Books
27 Maple Grove Estates
Swanton, Vermont 05488

ISBN 978-0-9903343-8-5

Acknowledgements

Several of the shorter essays and narratives in this collection were published in the Adirondack Mountain Club magazine, *Adirondac*. Others first appeared in *Blueline, Conservationist, Cybersoleil*, and *Palo Alto Review*.

Some have been taken from collections published by Wood Thrush Books: *Stalking the Sacred, Backcountry Excursions, Worldly Matters,* and *Loon Wisdom.*

"Greg's Waterfall" and "The Great Wild Silence" are chapter/essays in the book, *Cultivating the Wildness Within*, published by Red Dragonfly Press.

This is the first appearance of the longer narrative, "Deep Forest Ruminations."

Contents

Preface 7

The Allure of Mountains . . . 11

Snowshoeing in the High Peaks . . 18

Greg's Waterfall 27

Cutting Tracks into Hoffman Notch . . 34

Pilgrimage to Lost Pond . . . 41

Sampling the Real 75

An Exalted Dream 83

Mesmerized in Big Woods . . . 88

Loon Wisdom 93

The Great Wild Silence . . . 100

Immersed in Wildness . . . 106

Campfires and Bear Cans . . . 111

Deep Forest Ruminations . . . 116

Preface

As the opening essay in this collection suggests, I have been attracted to the Adirondacks ever since my move to Vermont in 1982, when I first saw those beautiful blue mountains looming over Lake Champlain. In the beginning I focused on the High Peaks, as most hikers do, scrambling up Mount Marcy, Haystack, the Wolfjaws, and other mountains in hot pursuit of the exhilarating feeling that one experiences on summits. But over time I turned more towards the sprawling wild forests to the south, where I could roam for days without seeing more than a handful of people, if anyone at all. There my thoughts roamed as freely as I did. And that is how the wild has seduced me, pure and simple, both in the Adirondacks and elsewhere.

The wild and all it entails is what I find most interesting as both a woods wanderer and philosopher, and what has been the subject of most of my writings during the past three decades. I find wildness just about everywhere: in parks, woodlots, fallow fields, roadside ditches, and my back yard, as well as in the forests and mountains of northern New England where I usually roam. But nowhere does it speak to me as loudly and clearly as it does in the West Canada Lakes Wilderness and places like it in the Adirondacks. So I keep going back there, in search of the deep connection with nature that I crave, and for answers to the most profound questions that we as human beings ask ourselves.

The primary object of his collection is to convey the experiences and accompanying thoughts I had while camped alone for five days at Pillsbury Lake in the summer of 2017. To do that effectively, I realized that those thoughts and experiences had to be put in context. That is what the dozen short pieces leading up to "Deep Forest Ruminations" are all about. It makes little sense to talk about "staying put" until a long history of woods wandering has been firmly established. Besides, woods wandering and staying put are interconnected. What I thought and did at Pillsbury Lake is rooted in the thoughts and experiences that I have enjoyed during all my deep woods excursions through the years.

The pieces in this book are laid out chronologically, more or less, thus making it easier for the reader to follow my evolution as a philosopher of wildness. This also makes it easier to follow my love affair with deep woods, and how that has unfolded over time. There is redundancy here, certainly, as some experiences are mentioned repeatedly. My brief sojourn at West Lake, for example, is touched upon several times. This is a good thing, I think. The most difficult concepts must be approached from several different angles to be fully understood. The word "mystical" comes to mind. It's not easy speaking about the unspeakable, but that's exactly what I try to do.

While these essays and short narratives have been brought together to shed some light on my personal philosophy of wildness, I hope that they also draw attention to the wonder and beauty of that wide-open country in upstate New York. Each piece is, first and foremost, a celebration of the natural world as I have encountered it inside the Blue Line. And like my full-length narrative about hiking the Northville-Placid Trail, *The Allure of Deep Woods*, I hope this book warrants a place in the literature of the Adirondacks. That is, I hope lovers of Adirondack wildness enjoy reading it for many years to come. If it inspires others to have their own backcountry adventures, or if it enhances the experiences they've already had, well, that's even better.

Walt McLaughlin
June 2018

THE GREAT WILD
SILENCE

The Allure of Mountains

Walking along a bike path on a sunny spring day, I gaze across the placid waters of Lake Champlain and into the cold blue mountains known as the Adirondacks. They dominate the horizon, suggesting that they might spread westward forever. They rise from the planet's surface like a blister on inflamed skin, teasing once-and-future climbers like myself with snow-capped summits and icy slides. At the heart of them rises the Great Range. Behind the lofty peaks of the Great Range, a white pyramid protrudes from the skyline like the tip of an iceberg floating in dark Atlantic waters. That's the topmost portion of Mt. Marcy. I suppress a vague, feverish desire to drop everything and race towards it like some crazed pilgrim.

A little over a month ago, I went up Mt. Marcy with four friends. I fought a frigid wind causing near white out conditions until it scored a technical knockout. I drove my tired, aching body over the glazed rocks above tree line in a final push for the summit, until one of my companions convinced me that the climb wasn't worth the gray patch of frostbite that the wind would leave on my face. Right now, frostbite seems implausible. In late April, the Adirondacks look like oversized hills only a few miles away. But mountains are never as close or as facile as they appear.

Two years ago, I hiked over Mt. Marcy with relative ease, following a boyhood friend up a well-beaten path. We had wisely chosen late summer to take on the mountains. Even with full backpacks straining at our shoulders, the ascent required little more than half a day's effort and a little sweat. The hike from Slant Rock Shelter to the top of Haystack Mountain the following day was even easier. Still, I couldn't help but wonder why we were pushing ourselves this way. For the satisfaction of attaining a goal? For the exercise? For the view? Those are the reasons that most hikers give when you press them, but none seems reason enough to ascend great mounds of rock rising into the sky. Surely there must be a more profound driving force behind it all.

Many outdoor enthusiasts scorn mountain climbing, arguing that a preoccupation with mountain summits detracts from the subtle, more wondrous aspects of wild nature. John Burroughs was no stranger to the Adirondacks, but he preferred the lesser hills around his Catskill home. Thoreau is quite famous for his meandering walks – most of which never took him beyond the relatively flat ground surrounding Concord. Whitman wrote his most eloquent descriptions of nature while lounging under a tree in his back yard. It appears that the great, mountainous wilds explored by Verplanck Colvin, Bob Marshall and John Muir is not necessary for a deep appreciation of nature. So why bother with them?

A few years back, my brother and I hiked several days in the Adirondacks without once stepping above the tree line. We did a tour of the most notable gaps in the High Peaks Region: Indian Pass, Algonquin Pass and Avalanche Pass. Not once did we even attempt a summit. I was ready to climb some rocky protrusion, but my brother was happy enough to ramble through lowlands, enjoying waterfalls, glistening streams and deep woods quiet. So I followed his lead and found myself thoroughly enjoying them as well. Still, we were the exception rather than the rule on those trails. During our short trek, we passed scores of more goal-oriented hikers headed for one summit or another. In the High Peaks Region, bagging peaks is the thing to do.

Growing up in the gently rolling hills of Ohio, I often dreamt of climbing high, faraway mountains. So I headed out West as soon as I turned eighteen. I saw plenty of awe-inspiring mountains during that excursion, but another six years would pass before I would grab an ice axe and actually struggle to the top of one. It finally happened while I was living in Oregon. I enrolled in an alpine school, which amounted to four days of rock and snow climbing clinics in the Three Sisters Wilderness. The training culminated in an all-day climb up Broken Top, a lesser-known peak in the Cascade Range.

Looming several thousand feet above our base camp like an unapproachable god, Broken Top looked ominous, indeed. In the middle of June, its broad shoulders were still covered with snow. A small glacier nestled in its lap. The ascent took six hours. The final leg of the ascent was a roped climb up a steep, intimidating pitch on the north face of the mountain.

The 2,000-foot drop over my left shoulder to the blinding white glacier below made me realize just how crazy one must be to engage in this sport. But for some inexplicable reason, I loved every second of that death-defying climb – as if nothing in the whole world could possibly be more fulfilling.

"What is the problem of Everest?" Sir John Hunt asks in his book, *The Conquest of Everest*, as if scrawling the question across a classroom blackboard. Then he describes in great detail how his climbing party put the first two men, Hillary and Tensing, on top of the world's highest mountain. It is hard to imagine a more riveting subject matter, yet the book is dull reading by most people's standards. That's because only a climber can sustain interest in the tedious preparations and complex logistics that make such a climb successful. Hunt frames "the problem" as well as anyone can. The trick is to enter a realm utterly hostile to life, then return home in one piece. In that respect, his book clearly illustrates how analytical, how methodical, how thoroughly organized a good climbing expedition must be. But one has to wonder... To what end?

"Because it is there," Mallory, a renowned British mountaineer, replied when asked why he climbed mountains. In that famous yet deceptively simple response lurks the paradox of mountain climbing. Even the experienced climber doesn't fully understand why he or she does it. Or perhaps the reason is too embarrassing for words, too irrational to justify the altogether rational approach that an experienced climber must take in order to achieve the desired goal. Any fool can run up a mountain unprepared, but only a thinking, well-organized climber gets up there and back in relative safety. The method seems to contradict the urge.

The feats of climbers are considered acts of heroism by many, as if valor could be demonstrated on an icy precipice just as easily as on a battlefield. Think of the climber as a hero in the classical sense. As Ernest Becker pointed out in his book, *The Denial of Death*: "The hero [in ancient times] was the man who could go into the spirit world, the world of the dead, and return alive." What better place to do that than upon a forbidding mountaintop?

The summit is where Father Sky and Mother Earth meet. It is the confluence of corporeal and incorporeal worlds, of heaven and here/now. The summit of Mt. Sinai is where Moses went to receive the commandments. The Greek gods ruled the world from atop Mt. Olympus. What classical hero hasn't wrestled with the gods, confronted death? Is it any wonder, then, that the world's greatest climbers are held in such high esteem?

Some would argue that mountain climbing is altogether too Western, too yang and not enough yin, too self-aggrandizing and arrogant. Lao Tzu, the father of Taoism, certainly wouldn't have approved of it. "The highest good is that of water," he states in the *Tao Te Ching*. Water, not rock. The gentle downward flow of things in sync with the forces of gravity, not a forceful thrusting upward, against nature. No doubt the founders of the world's other great religious traditions would have agreed. The Buddhist works hard to diminish self-importance; the Hindu knows his place in the world; the Moslem praises the greatness of Allah, not human endeavor. Jesus of Nazareth preached time and again the importance of humility. The meek shall inherit the earth, not the conquistadors. The urge to stand godlike and victorious upon a mountain summit runs against the grain of conventional religious sentiment. So one is left wondering: where does this urge come from?

It appears that humankind is of two minds about mountains. In her book, *Mountain Gloom and Mountain Glory*, Marjorie Hope Nicholson shows how the ancient Greek writers revered mountains, while the Romans harbored negative feelings about them. This tension persists throughout literary history. During the Middle Ages, mountains were often used as symbols for the dark side of human nature. But later on, the Romantic poets lauded mountains as bastions of the sublime. Is a mountaintop the throne of God or a vortex of sinister, gothic forces? Does climbing mountains desecrate the sacred or celebrate it? It all depends upon whom you ask.

Rene Daumal addressed the matter directly in his unfinished manuscript, *Mount Analogue*. He tried to fuse East with West, the spiritual with the mundane, the rational with the mystical. In his novel, a two-fold approach to the archetypal mountain quickly takes shape. "Its summit must be inaccessible, but its base accessible," Daumal explains, "It must be unique, and it must exist geographically. The door to the invisible must be made visible." Tall order. Deliberately confounding, some would say. Why would anyone aspire to climb a mountain so fundamentally unclimbable? Perhaps it doesn't matter whether or not Daumal's mountain is actually climbed. Perhaps the act of climbing is only meant as a metaphor for something else. Viewed in this light, it is easy to see every climbing expedition as an attempt *to go into the spirit world and return alive.*

It's not the climb, the endless blue sky overhead or the jagged mountain itself that I remember most about alpine school, but rather a point that the instructor kept making over and over: a smart climber knows when to go for the summit and when to abort. Last month, as I struggled up the icy, windblown shoulder of Mt. Marcy, well above the tree line yet still light years away from the top, I made the right decision when I chose to turn back. Yet there's a part of me that wishes I'd gone all the way, no matter what.

Looking across the lake one last time, I pick out all the High Peaks I've climbed over the years: East Dix, Algonquin, Hurricane and others. Then I turn towards home, wondering if maybe I should stop climbing. What difference does any ascent make in the greater scheme of things? As a rational creature, I feel a need to fully understand this urge to risk everything on a mountain, so that I can either surrender myself to it or squelch it once and for all. But that's impossible. There are too many factors involved here, too many conflicting beliefs. Besides, the deepest human impulses rarely make sense in the light of reason alone. So all I can do is climb, then stand mute on top of the world, exhausted and awestruck, basking in the wonder of it all, while the urge that puts me there remains forever shrouded in mystery.

Snowshoeing in the High Peaks

What can a hiker do in late winter when there are several feet of snow on the ground? The answer to that question might seem obvious to anyone who has grown up in the North Country, but it took me a while to catch on. Just recently, I've learned that mid-March can be an excellent time of year to get outdoors even though everything is still covered with great piles of the white stuff. Just recently, I've discovered snowshoeing. Since I've never felt comfortable on skis, snowshoes have become a viable alternative to staying indoors and going stir crazy. You could say that I've taken up the sport out of sheer necessity.

Although I'm still a novice when it comes to snowshoeing, I joined my friend, Steve, and five other Vermonters at the Garden Parking Lot one Sunday morning for a three-day trek into the High Peaks. Planning the trip well in advance, Steve had reserved an ADK cabin halfway up the Johns Brook Valley for a couple nights. That made it possible for us to stay in the mountains without all the gear necessary for winter camping. When Steve asked me if I wanted to go, I said yes, absolutely. I jumped at the chance to enjoy nature in winter for more than just a few hours at a time.

After strapping the last few pieces of stray gear onto our packs with bungee cords, we started up the trail in twos and threes. Those with cross-country skis quickly forged ahead while the rest of us brought up the rear, plodding along on snowshoes. The sky was solidly overcast but no wind stirred. The air temperature held in the mid-twenties. It was a perfect day to be in the woods. Since no major changes in weather had been predicted for the next few days, we looked forward to mounting the Great Range during our trip.

Our two-hour jaunt to the cabin was relatively easy despite packs heavily laden with food and supplies. The snow underfoot was a solid, hard-packed surface all the way. Cross-country skiing remains a popular winter sport in the North Country and there's been a sudden surge of interest in snowshoeing lately. As a result, the trail we followed had been packed by scores of backcountry travelers who had gone before us.

We must have passed a dozen groups on their way out – far more people than we'd see during the rest of our outing. Timing is everything. Since we were starting our trip when most people were finishing theirs, we would have the Adirondacks largely to ourselves over the next couple days. A mass exodus was well underway by the time Steve, Jim and I had gone a mile from the parking lot. By the time we reached the cabin, most of the weekenders had cleared out of the area altogether.

Lunch was almost over when I straggled into the cabin a half hour behind the seasoned skiers in our group. An unfolded topo map covered the table and everyone was talking about a quick dash up the Great Range that afternoon. Which summit? Which route? Being a dozen pounds overweight and new to winter travel, I was a bit daunted by the prospect of climbing any mountain that afternoon. I thought we were going to rest up for a big climb the following day, but my companions convinced me that fair weather is a rare event in the mountains this time of year. Go when you can. I wolfed down a sandwich and followed everyone else out the door. A consensus had been reached. Saddleback was the most accessible peak.

Some people survive the cold season simply by hunkering down, keeping close to the hearth. They wait patiently for spring. Growing up in Ohio, that's what I used to do, anyhow. But winter is long in the North Country, so I changed my survival strategy a few years after moving here. I quickly learned to get outdoors whenever the opportunity arose. I went hiking whenever I thought the snow was crusted over enough to support my weight. Unfortunately, I was usually wrong about the condition of the snow's surface. More often than not, I would slog my way to exhaustion, post-holing through several feet of the white stuff for a mile or so before calling it quits. Since wading through snow isn't exactly my idea of fun, I investigated other modes of winter travel. Eventually, I came around to the only practical alternative to those long, thin, slippery boards called skis: I rented some snowshoes.

My first experience on snowshoes was pleasant enough, but cutting a new trail through fresh snow turned out to be a lot more work than I thought it would be. My second outing, along a well-groomed trail after a gentle overnight snowfall, occurred on a sunny day when the air was so still that I could hear a bird singing a mile away. I floated through deep green hemlocks casting blue shadows across pure white powder. I marveled at tree trunks etched sharply against the sky – vivid brown and dark gray lines in dazzling light. Epiphany! In an instant I converted to the cult of snowshoeing. Before the last of the snow melted that season, I had my own pair.

There are several different kinds of snowshoes on the market these days. The most popular variety is a short, narrow, plastic-and-aluminum snowshoe with metal claws underneath to grip icy surfaces or hard-packed snow. This somewhat expensive, high-tech snowshoe can be found in most mountain shops. They're all the rage. While they aren't particularly effective in deep powder, they work quite well on the hard-packed trails that most winter travelers tend to use. On the other hand, old timers still cling to the traditional snowshoe – the kind made with wood and rawhide. This variety usually shows up at flea markets and yard sales during the summer. Because they're much longer and wider than the newer snowshoes, they work better on flat or rolling terrain covered with deep powder. Unfortunately, they're not particularly effective on steep, icy slopes.

My snowshoes are called Green Mountain Bear Paws. They're manufactured by an outfit in Stowe, Vermont. Being a hybrid snowshoe, they're long enough to support my weight in deep powder, yet narrow enough for the trails. Since they're made with traditional materials, rawhide and wood, they suit my old fashioned tastes as well. It's a good all-purpose snowshoe – ideal for guys like me who want to go everywhere.

Monday morning, day two. We were on the move again. One member of our group stayed behind at the cabin – his knees having taken all the punishment they could handle while coming down Saddleback. The rest of us headed for the summit of Mt. Haystack – six miles away and three thousand feet above the cabin. The Rose brothers, along with a couple others in our group, had attempted Haystack the previous winter but had been forced back by sub-zero temperatures and high winds. This time there were no such obstacles. The temperature remained in the high twenties. No wind blew. A couple inches of fresh snow had accumulated overnight but no one seemed too concerned about it. We were confident about reaching the summit that day. The group was confident, that is. Personally, I wasn't quite sure if I was equal to the task. The first day's effort had taken a great deal out of me.

We moved up the trail mostly without words, reserving our energy for the task at hand. Deep snow transformed the low roar of the brook to a murmur. Bird songs were few and far between. The *skrunch, skrunch* of our snowshoes seemed unnaturally loud. The clean intensity of the cold air reaching deep into my lungs made me feel more alert than I thought possible in the end of winter. Month number five of the cold season and still it maintained some of its original allure. I was amazed by it. A few more outings like this and my generally negative attitude towards winter might fade away completely.

Snowshoes were as much a part of the aboriginal way of life in these Northeastern woodlands as the birch bark canoe. The first people migrating to North America from Siberia thousands of years ago brought snowshoes with them. The first Europeans to use snowshoes were probably Vikings scratching out a living along the frozen Labrador coast. In the 17th Century, French Canadian voyageurs traversing the subarctic and Englishmen trading around the Hudson Bay no doubt learned about snowshoes from Cree and Algonquin peoples. The Abenaki and the Iroquois probably introduced snowshoes to the English settlers of New England and New York. Roger's Rangers – that renowned band of New Hampshire militiamen – employed snowshoes during the French and Indian War. In March of 1758, they fought the French and their Algonquin allies in the Lake George region of the Adirondacks atop four feet of snow in what's now known as the Battle of Snowshoes.

As the bird flies, Lake George is only forty miles southeast of the Johns Brook Valley. As the six of us slowly, arduously worked our way up the Great Range, the French and Indian War seemed light years away. Yet we propelled ourselves over the snow the same way Native Americans and frontiersmen had done for centuries.

Haystack isn't easily accessible. From any direction, it's a long hike to the top. At 3,500 feet, I started losing steam. Just above 4,000 feet, I felt a spasm in my left thigh. After negotiating a rather steep pitch just below Little Haystack, my leg began to cramp. That was the end of the climb for me. The rest of the group seemed no less exhausted, but somehow they were all able to keep going. I assured Steve that I'd be all right, ambling slowly back down the trail by myself towards the cabin. He assured me that he and the others would be on my heels shortly. With that justification, I did what I had wanted to do since our departure from the parking lot the day before: I cut away from the group for an hour or so of luxurious backcountry solitude.

A great deal of snow had fallen during the previous two months. Not quite record-breaking amounts but getting there. On our way up the Great Range, trail markers nailed to trees six feet above the ground had sunken into the snow. I rediscovered them on my way down, along with the semblance of a hard-packed trail. All around me the green boughs of conifers drooped with the weight of wet snow. Stopping to catch my breath, I noticed the absolute silence of the forest. Only the occasional snap of a dry twig or the muffled thump of snow landing upon snow compromised it.

The tracks of snowshoe hares crisscrossed the trail for miles, convincing me that they were enjoying a banner year. Evidently, their predators can't get around nearly as well in such deep powder. A woodpecker knocked on a dead tree; the swollen buds of hobblebush and moosewood protruded through the snow. Spring wasn't far away. The tiny cones of great hemlocks have been strewn across the snow's surface like woody dice. The lonely call of a chickadee, a song quite common in these mountains even in deep winter, suddenly sounded to me like the harbinger of a new season. The gurgle of hidden rivulets carrying snowmelt down the Johns Brook seemed like another sure sign of imminent transition. I sweated even as I eased gradually downhill. The day grew warmer with air temperatures threatening to break the freezing mark. Suddenly it dawned on me that this would probably be my last snowshoeing trip the season. The snow would soon melt away. For the first time ever, I felt a tinge of sadness at the prospect of spring. Getting outdoors regularly on snowshoes was changing my perspective on things.

That evening in camp, the faces gathered around the dinner table were all glazed over with fatigue. To my mild surprise, I suddenly realized that I had more energy left than anyone else. So I grabbed the buckets to fetch water for cooking and cleaning. The cut in the snow down by the brook was at least four feet deep. I approached it warily. The Johns Brook flowed steadily beneath the snow. I couldn't help but wonder how Native Americans survived winter as well as they did when even fetching water required a good deal of effort and caution. Perhaps one simply grows accustomed to such minor, daily ordeals.

Later on that night, I slipped outside once again to look for stars among the trees and catch an earful of that incredible deep-woods silence. In the summer, the Adirondacks seem almost tame. But on dark winter nights like this one, when a Great Unknown prevails in the forest, these mountains seem utterly wild. Although the air was still, I could hear the wind howling through high mountain passes many miles away. When the distant wind subsided, I held my breath to keep from being distracted by the sound of my own breathing as I listened even more intently. Cold, dark, stillness… It was quiet enough for me to hear the trees creaking even though they were hardly moving.

On our way out the next day, we passed half a dozen young men on their way to Slant Rock Shelter. They marched up the mountain in blatant disregard for the contrariness of winter weather. They had neither skis nor snowshoes. Granted, the trail was packed well enough to walk upon, but a quick thaw could quickly turn the hard snow beneath their feet to slush. A whiteout could make even a well-marked trail difficult to follow in broad daylight.

It's amazing how quickly I've come to rely upon my snowshoes. Now I can't imagine being without them. And while I still prefer the roughest hike through hot, heavily vegetated woodlands to an easy trek across open snowfields, I'm quick to take advantage of any opportunity I get to strap on my 'shoes. Without a doubt, snowshoeing requires a great deal more effort than hiking or skiing, but it's a mode of winter travel that suits guys like me quite well. A slow, steady, resolute moving forward... Snowshoes make it possible to go just about anywhere during winter – the more snow the better.

Greg's Waterfall

During a short, overnight trip into the Vermont woods, my brother Greg told me that he would like to try a much longer excursion into the wild. This surprised me. We had discussed the matter before but I didn't think he was serious. After all, Greg isn't exactly the outdoorsy type. He's more of a house cat and cardigan sweater kind of guy. I assumed that he went with me into the woods the same way I went with him to antique shops – only to spend time with his brother. After all, he had moved to Vermont less than a year earlier and we were just getting to know each other as adults. But there was a look in his eyes that convinced me that he really did want this, that the fire of wildness had been ignited within him. So we made plans for a five-day trek together through the High Peaks region of the Adirondacks.

Since Greg was interested more in lakes and streams than mountain vistas, we planned our trip accordingly. Most people venture into the mountains to bag peaks, but Greg isn't most people. We would stay low, hiking along waterways, crossing over higher ground only when we had to. That was okay by me. It struck me as a novel and interesting approach to the

High Peaks – one that would force me to see the region in a different way. Besides, I didn't want to push Greg too hard. I still wasn't sure that he was up for the rigors of an extended backcountry outing.

A hot afternoon in the end of August. We got a late start that day, thanks to some pressing business that Greg had to do first. We reached Adirondak Loj at two, parked our car then set foot upon a trail headed south towards Indian Pass. The heat was oppressive and our packs were heavy so we took our time, stopping frequently. We hiked and sweated all afternoon, encountering too many other hikers along the way to have anything like a wilderness experience. We tramped through a series of mud holes as the trail skirted Scott Clearing then finally made camp along a feeder stream tumbling down from Algonquin Peak. Sundown came fast. Too tired to build a campfire, we cooked up dinner on my camp stove. We had barely enough time to eat before darkness enveloped us. Then we slung our food by flashlight and settled in for the night.

Around four a.m., Greg noticed flashes of light through the trees. That gave us a chance to secure our camp before the storm hit. We stayed relatively dry inside my tent but a light rain escalated to a downpour soaking our gear outside. Greg had a blister on one foot and an eyelid swollen half-shut from a bug bite. Taking all this into consideration, we agreed that it would be best to sit tight for a day. After all, we had plenty of time and there was nowhere in particular that we had to be.

After securing our streamside camp, we grabbed a few essentials then day-hiked to Indian Pass. It took less than an hour to get there. We went as far as Summit Rock then turned around. The summer heat persisted. At one point during the hike, I stopped to wet my hair beneath a trickle running down the sheer rock opposite Wallface Mountain. Greg did the same, leaning into it, letting the icy ribbon of water soak his head thoroughly. A wild baptism. I smiled. Yeah, now he was getting into it. Evidently, Greg has an affinity for water. This makes sense. He has always been a go-with-the-flow kind of guy.

Up at daybreak, our third day out, I slipped out of the tent as quietly as possible. Greg gave me a dirty look then rolled over. I puttered about camp for well over an hour before my sleepy-eyed brother arose. The heat wave had broken, as promised by weather forecasters a few days earlier, and I was looking forward to the climb up and over Algonquin Pass in the cool morning air. Greg pondered the matter at length over coffee and a cigarette. Then he rallied. We broke camp and headed out.

The climb wasn't too arduous. We reached the top of the pass by midday and were soon on our way downhill. I talked up the wonder and beauty of deep woods but Greg seemed rather skeptical – until we reached water again, that is. While standing on the footbridge that separates Lake Colden from the Flowed Land, something came over him. Mount Colden rose dramatically from the rippled lake. Algonquin Peak loomed just west of it. The deep cut between them made it clear where Avalanche Lake was hiding. Aside from the ranger station we had passed, there was nothing but wild country around us. Greg was impressed. We lingered long enough for him to absorb it all.

Late that afternoon, we crept up an eroded, muddy trail hugging the Opalescent River. We were tired, dirty and menaced by bugs. Our shoulders ached from the weight of our packs. That didn't prevent us from enjoying the Flume, though. Other waterfalls appeared during our steady ascent. Despite a mutual desire to get somewhere and make camp, we stopped several times to enjoy the sight, sound and smell of tumbling water. One waterfall in particular caught Greg's eye. We lingered there long enough for him to smoke a cigarette. Whitewater roared over stone to a pool occupied by a fallen tree. Greg lost himself in it. In fact, he was so mesmerized by the cascading water that I didn't dare say a word. All I could do was stand back and wait. When finally he was finished communing with the waterfall, we shouldered our packs one last time and finished the day's walk.

Everyone has his or her own way of grooving with the wild. For some it comes on a mountaintop. Others are delighted when a furry creature shows itself. Still others become ecstatic when a rare bird or wildflower suddenly appears. I have seen grown men and women awestruck by a sunset while fishing a remote pond at dusk. I have watched urbanites become slack-jawed over the simplest things: a beaver swimming in a backwoods pond, conifers creaking incessantly in the wind, or the way the light reflects off the dewdrops dangling from a spider's web. I have experienced many such moments myself.   But a wild epiphany is something else.

A wild epiphany is something deeply personal. It's much harder to understand.   It comes without warning, and the person experiencing it may not be fully aware of its impact until much later. Who's to say how profound any particular encounter is or how it can change a person?   No one can, certainly, yet there are times when each and every one of us is suddenly unhinged by the natural world – when the planet stops spinning for a nanosecond and one *connects*. For those of us who have guided others into the wild, it's a marvelous thing to behold.

Not more than a mile beyond the Flume, Greg and I made camp.   We chose a spot next to the Opalescent River where the stream veers out of sight from the trail. We set up the tent on a tiny patch of flat earth surrounded by spruces.   Then we gathered wood.   A swarm of black flies drove us into the tent for a while, but the cool air of early evening eventually sent them to ground.   Greg tended a campfire on the stream's rocky shoreline while I fixed dinner.   A gibbous moon rose into the sky as the sun retired for the day.   After we had eaten dinner, Greg cracked a few jokes then suddenly fell silent.

"What's wrong?" I asked.

Greg told me that he felt funny.   Then he struggled for the right words to describe the thoughts and feelings churning deep within.   He said it was strange being camped here in the middle of nowhere, away from the trail, and that he had felt different ever since we had crossed that footbridge back at Lake

Colden. "It's like another world out here," he said while looking around.

I couldn't help but smile. "You're in the wild now, " I responded, as if that explained everything. Then we both fell silent, letting a crackling campfire do all the talking.

In the morning, I pored over maps while Greg slowly awakened. When I thought the time was right for it, I proposed that we continue going uphill, climbing over Mt. Marcy before heading back towards Adirondak Loj. But Greg had another idea. He proposed that we go back the way we came and stop by that waterfall again. After all, we had been too tired the day before to fully appreciate it. Hmm. While that wasn't my first choice, I had no objection. Greg knew what he wanted. Who was I to stand in his way? He was getting into it – that was the main thing. I didn't really care where we went or what we did. So we packed up and headed out the same way we had come.

Another long waterfall sitting, another cigarette. To be honest, I didn't quite get it. I couldn't groove on falling water with the same intensity that Greg did. Then again, I didn't have to. It was his moment in the wild, not mine.

Our hike out was pleasant enough. We meandered along the shoreline of Lake Colden and Avalanche Lake, walked up through Avalanche Pass, and made camp at Kagel Lean-to. A cloudburst delayed our departure from that shelter on the fifth day, but that only gave us time to talk and get to know each other better. And when finally the rain did let up, we were something more than brothers. Suddenly we were friends with a shared past. Fifth day out, we had dropped our shields. So it goes when two people spend enough time together in wild country.

In Lake Placid that afternoon, we enjoyed hot sandwiches and cold beer while lounging on a restaurant deck overlooking the water. We were a little self-conscious about being grungy, but the waitress was kind enough to ignore it. While sitting at that restaurant, Greg experienced wilderness withdrawal for the very first time. He commented about all the noise and bustle around us, making more of an observation than registering a complaint. That made me laugh. I assured him that it was normal to notice such things after being in deep woods for a while. During the drive home, we talked at length about the outing, reliving the highs and lows of it while laughing a lot. But Greg's few precious moments at that waterfall were no laughing matter. Some encounters in the wild take on the weight of religion, going beyond mere sentiment or words.

Cutting Tracks into Hoffman Notch

Stepping off the road just after a chilly sunrise, I lift my leg high enough to clear the iced bank left by a passing snowplow, then press my snowshoe into pristine powder. Peering through the defoliated trees, I can barely make out the northern ends of the two most commanding features of the Hoffman Notch Wilderness: Blue Ridge and Washburn Ridge. Between them lie Hornet Cobbles and Hoffman Notch. I have never been there before. I head that direction, telling myself that I can follow a south/southeast compass bearing to the Notch if the small clearing in the woods directly ahead isn't a trailhead. I cut a fresh set of tracks through virgin snow for about a minute before breathing a sigh of relief. There's an Adirondack Mountain Club trail marker nailed to a tree just a few yards beyond a closed gate.

Hiking alone into rarely traveled woods is never a good idea. Snowshoeing alone into them is downright foolhardy. But I have a special reserve of rationalizations to liberate me from the bonds of common sense whenever I've slipped into a mid-winter funk and the urge to commune with wild nature strikes hard and deep. Today's highly effective though somewhat lame rationalization: between the tracks I'm leaving in the snow and the trail markers on the trees, I'll be easy to find if someone has to come looking for me. Okay, so maybe the snowstorm due to hit this area later on today will obscure my tracks. No matter. The trail markers are unmistakable.

As I follow the trail markers through a copse of dark conifers, I cross the fresh tracks of both deer and snowshoe hares. There's no evidence that anyone else has come this way lately – not since the big storm five days ago. With each step I take, my snowshoes sink several inches into fine powder. Only a dusting of the white stuff covered the ground prior to that big storm, but now there's a foot and a half of it to slog through. That's enough to justify the cumbersome, rawhide-and-wood contraptions strapped to my boots.

Even though I break a sweat after only twenty minutes, post-holing this far without snowshoes would have had me gasping for air by now. As things are, there's a good chance that I'll be able to cut tracks all the way to Big Marsh Pond roughly three miles ahead. "Pace yourself," I whisper so that I don't disturb the wintry silence. Then I drop down to the flats separating the road from the northern door to the wilderness area.

The snow swishes underfoot each time I lift my snowshoe. My breathing is heavy. Cold air reaches deep into my lungs, forcing me to cough. A woodpecker knocks on a nearby tree so loudly that I don't recognize it at first. The sun illuminates tiny snowflakes gently falling to the ground from a partly cloudy sky. Long blue shadows crisscross the snow beneath a thinned stand of young birches. A slight breeze caresses my cheeks with its icy fingers.

I don't quite understand how this dormant world can heighten the senses, but it does. Nature in winter seems to be drawn with sharper lines. There's more contrast between light and dark, between color and its absence this time of year. Maybe it's the snow – the uniform substance covering over the overwhelming detail on the forest floor – that forces me to see the subtle differences.

I cross a brook, gingerly stepping across a tenuous snow-bridge between two short leads of open water. The brook appears to be no more than a half-foot deep but that doesn't diminish the dread I feel when the ice cracks underneath my snowshoes. I cross the brook a couple more times as I follow it into the Notch. With each crossing, I feel the same dread. As I jump from one boulder to another, across a rather deep, narrow and fast-moving torrent, I wonder how quickly I could build a fire. Since the air temperature is somewhere in the teens, getting my feet wet wouldn't be that big a deal. I'd have plenty of time to dry them out before they froze. All the same, each brook crossing seems like a deepening of my commitment to the wild.

Funny how relatively minor risks accumulate, unnoticeable at first, until they pose a real threat. A backcountry traveler is always something of a gambler, taking his or her chances with the natural elements. But, as every gambler knows, the house wins if you stay at the gaming table long enough. A smart gambler knows when to get out.

The trail into Hoffman Notch becomes difficult to follow as the understory becomes cluttered with hobblebush. I can't help but wonder how many hikers pound this trail during the summer. From this perspective it's hard to say. There's enough snow on the ground to obscure the beaten path from view. Consequently, I use the trail markers to thread my way through the brush. Since the trail is probably the easiest route through the Notch, I try to stay on or near it as the ravine narrows. I'm getting enough of a workout cutting fresh tracks up the steady incline. No sense making things any harder than they have to be.

Going through Hoffman Notch is rather anticlimactic. The steep ridges on either side of me draw towards each other, then spread apart. Spotting an icefall hanging from to a rocky face of the western ridge, I tell myself that I'm passing through the gap in the mountains. But not until the ground underfoot levels out a quarter hour later does it really feel that way.

Exhausted after three miles of hard travel, I begin to wonder if maybe I should turn back. I look at my watch. It's only mid-morning. Most of the day still lies ahead so I keep going. The pond can't be far away. I assure myself that I'll pull out my foam pad and take a well-deserved break once I reach it.

The Adirondacks are particularly attractive to people like me who live in the northwestern corner of Vermont. Wandering along the shoreline of Lake Champlain, I often gaze longingly at those cold blue mountains. Because the Green Mountains are in my backyard, I explore them much more than I do the Adirondacks. But that only heightens the mystery of those rocky sentinels across the lake. Never mind all those outrageously inexpensive flights to southern climes in mid-winter. Give me a full tank of gas, a small box of granola bars, and a fair-weather window wide enough for a daytrip to upstate New York's snow-covered mountains. The chill in the air feels right to me. The wood smoke curling from cabins along frozen lakes and ponds smells like home, even though my own rooms are heated with gas. I don't want to live in a world that is always green and warm and sunny. If I did, I would have moved south a long time ago.

Big Marsh Pond is much larger in real life than it seems on my topo map. And colder, too. A steady wind races across the frozen pond, quickly numbing my face as I skirt snowdrifts along the edge of the ice. I take cover in dense spruce. Lunch is a frigid affair despite the foam pad I fashion into a seat and the thermos of hot water I have brought with me. I wolf down as much food as I can stomach to keep the internal fire stoked. My exposed hands quickly freeze in the process. I switch hands as I eat, moving them in and out of my mitts. That only staves off the inevitable a few extra minutes.

A solitary blue jay cries out. Directly in front of me, Hoffman Mountain looms over the pond – a dark blue mound laced with fresh snow. It remains somewhat aloof from the closer peaks living in its shadow. I am suddenly overwhelmed by a surprising sensation: joy mixed with dread. I have felt this way before, in other wild places at other times. Although I'm only three miles from the nearest road, the cold intensity of this high valley makes that distance seem much farther. It's as if I'm in the heart of wild-ness itself. The sensation is delightful *because* it's so terrifying. I want to stay here all day and soak up the harsh beauty of this place until my food and hot water run out. I want to feel the cold hand of nature pressing hard against my chest, but I'm dangerously alone and my right foot has already started freezing. I have been here three quarters of an hour already. Time to go. I stuff a few remaining granola bars in my shirt pocket then stomp back down the trail to get the circulation going in my right foot again.

A few minutes down the trail, I start to realize just how exhausted I am. Cutting tracks to the pond took more out of me than expected. The muscles in my legs and lower back are pretty much spent. Fortunately, I am retracing the tracks that I cut earlier, thus conserving what little energy I have left. Going back down the trail is easy enough but it's nearly impossible to step back into my vigorous, early-morning tracks as I cross the flats. By early afternoon I'm completely played out. With a smile rising to my lips, I spot my car through the thinning trees. Then I exit the woods.

After a long drive home, I hobble indoors with snowshoes in hand and a rucksack slung over my slumped shoulder. When my wife gets home from work, she asks me how I'm doing. She's wondering, no doubt, if I have left my mid-winter funk in the woods. I am tired, very tired, I tell her. She considers this good news.

Three days later, I'm slipping into a funk again but it's not nearly as deep as it was before I went to the Notch. I stop in the middle of a work project to pore over topo maps. There's a big blank spot in the Adirondacks just west of the High Peaks. I'd like to go there someday. There's another place on an isolated, northeastern slope of the Green Mountains, a bit closer to home. Haven't been there before, either. I wonder what the weather will be like the day after tomorrow.

Pilgrimage to Lost Pond

1

Right after the road changes from pavement to dirt, I spot something moving through the woods to my left. A deer drifts through a sunny glade then slips back into forest shadows. I slam on the brakes. A cloud of dust envelops my old pickup truck. I snap my fingers to get the attention of the German shepherd dog sitting next to me, but she's too busy sniffing the air – head out the passenger window. By the time Jesse turns her head towards me, the deer has disappeared into the foliage. No matter. Spotting the deer is a good omen. I step on the accelerator, finishing the ten-mile drive from the main highway to Wakely Dam. Just beyond the dam, another mile and a half up the narrowing road, I find a turnout next to an easily overlooked trailhead. There I leave the truck and commence a weeklong trek, hiking southward into one of the largest roadless areas in the Adirondacks: the West Canada Lakes Wilderness.

My pack is heavy but I don't care. I've waited two years for this moment – it taking that long for me to break out of my regular routine. With walking stick firmly in hand, I charge down the trail. Jesse falls behind immediately. Old dog on her last leg, she's been

41

having a hard time keeping up with me lately. The heat of a sultry August afternoon doesn't help matters. So I cut my pace to match hers. This could very well be Jesse's last big outing. I want to make sure that it's a good one for her.

A half hour into the hike, I stop at a campsite on the Cedar River Flow. The Flow is a long, shallow body of water created by Wakely Dam a few miles north. Deer flies have been chewing up Jesse's ears worse than usual so I apply some bug dope to them. Afterwards, I walk down to the water's edge for a good look at the reedy lake. Jesse wades a few yards out to soak her belly while gulping down the cool, clear water – her thick coat holds the heat. A solitary loon calls in the distance, as if to welcome me and my four-legged companion to the wild. And the stress of the four-hour drive from home to trailhead this morning quickly dissipates.

West Canada Lake is roughly fifteen miles from the trailhead. It's located right in the middle of a sprawling forest. With a good path underfoot, I could easily reach it in two days. But taking my dog's poor health into consideration, I think I'll do it in three. There's no rush. I have eight days to get there and back, doing whatever comes naturally in the process. I've done enough backpacking to know how to get the most out of an outing. My hardcore trekking days are behind me. Since hiking Vermont's Long Trail end-to-end several years back, I've had a change of heart. Now it's all about being in the woods, not just passing through them.

The Northville/Lake Placid Trail is fairly well marked and easy to follow despite being overgrown in places. It isn't used much, compared to that network of cattle-paths crisscrossing the High Peaks. There aren't many 4,000-foot peaks located near this meandering, 130-mile trail and that, I suppose, is what keeps it from being overrun. The Northville/Lake Placid Trail begins in the southwestern corner of the Adirondack Park, winds northward through boggy, relatively flat country before turning slightly east at Long Lake. From there the trail cuts along the western edge of the High Peaks to Lake Placid. There are plenty of lakes and ponds along the way. That's the main reason I'm on it. I want to ply backcountry waters for trout while enjoying Adirondack wildness. I have a fly rod as well as a compass and intend to put both to good use.

Closed gentian and meadowsweet grow in abundance along the trail as it passes through shady forest groves and patches of sun-drenched grass. Here the Northville/Lake Placid Trail follows an old woods road. But the double track, wide enough to accommodate a jeep, disappears into a large wetland. On the other side of the wetland, a narrower path emerges. And trail markers appear more frequently. The heart of the wilderness can't be far away.

Not too far south of the wetland, I stumble into a trail junction. Turning down the side trail, I quickly reach the Cedar River Lean-To. Is the day's hike over already? Four miles isn't much of a trek, but it's enough for my dog the first day out. A family of canoeists paddle away just as Jesse and I appear in front of the shelter. I drop my pack and immediately start cleaning up the place. The shelter is full of brush. Half-charred pieces of green wood litter the ground all around the fire pit. Jesse goes down to the river to cool off.

Returning to camp, she collapses into the grass on the shady side of the shelter to watch me putter. I use a dull, rusty axe left at the shelter to split up the pieces of charred wood so they'll burn better.

One full hour of late-afternoon solitude, then I'm joined by three tired thru-hikers. They're doing the Northville/Lake Placid Trail end-to-end, from south to north. Oddly enough, the oldest of the three – a slender man in his 60s – is the least experienced. His son, Mark, has introduced him to backpacking. The third fellow, Jeff, is a thirty-something athlete who hooked up with them along the way. I push my things into a corner of the shelter, making room for them. They use that space to stash some of their gear then set up tents in tall grass. The untrammeled ground is softer there.

The older man, Fred, is a retired engineer. His son is a businessman. Jeff teaches grade school. And what do I do? I'm reluctant to say since my vocation has been something of a sore spot with me lately. "I'm a writer," I mutter, "But not a particularly successful one." Jeff asks why. Surprising myself, I blurt out the cold, hard truth of it: "I'm too much the philosopher and not enough of a wordsmith." As luck would have it, Jeff studied a lot of philosophy back in college so this disclosure excites him. He starts dropping "-Isms" all over the place, trying to pin one on me. From the way he fields provocative statements, I can tell that he's aching for a philosophical argument – the kind that people win or lose like boxing matches. I don't rise to his challenge at first, but eventually his rather casual comments about man and nature set me off. And before anyone is ready for it, I'm on a two-minute tirade about the authenticity of the wild and the absurdity of civilization.

"No, seriously now. Tell us what you *really* think," Fred says, trying to interject a little levity into the conversation. Jeff ignores the queue. Instead the young schoolteacher gives us all a lecture on the evils of technology as he fires up his camp stove. Dinnertime. I know better than to ruin a perfectly good meal with this kind of talk but can't help myself. I tell Jeff that I'm reluctant to discard tools – things such as knives, cooking pots and fire starters – that have proven to be so useful over the millennia.

"Sounds like you want it both ways," Jeff concludes, rather frustrated now by what he perceives as my evasiveness.

"I just don't buy into tidy, anti-technology credos, that's all," I respond, adding that I don't see any need for credos or the gurus who push them. Jeff is alarmed by this proclamation and I really should drop the matter, but I feel compelled to deliver a finishing blow: "Jesse is all the guru I need."

Am I joking? All three of the tired hikers stop what their doing and stare at me. The conversation is now in danger of really turning sour, so Jeff and I tacitly agree to change the subject. We start talking about food bartering on the trail, the trials and tribulations of thru-hiking – safe stuff like that. And the rest of the dinner hour is a much more pleasant affair.

After dinner, I grab my fly rod and go down to the river. I rig up while standing along the river's edge. Jesse joins me, finding a nice spot in the cool mud to lie down and watch. Mayflies hatch at dusk and a few fish rise to the dimpled surface, but I hook nothing. The fierce assaults of no-see-ums and mosquitoes make it difficult to concentrate. Or perhaps I'm still too upset about that dinnertime outburst of mine to focus upon what I'm doing. Either way, my fly-casting is fruitless.

For several months now, I've been trying to work up the courage to commit my worldview to paper. I feel a strong urge to write down my deepest thoughts on God, nature and humankind, but am convinced from the poor showing of my previous "think" pieces that no one wants to read stuff like that. In fact, I'm convinced that the best way to sink my already foundering literary career is to spout ideas that are neither popular nor easy to understand. I envy those with philosophies that are taken seriously – I've never been so fortunate. I despise those who tell others only what they want to hear; yet I see the practicality in it. Where does that leave me? Having to choose between intellectual dishonesty and literary suicide. Not the best place to be.

I glance at the clouds gathering along the dark horizon, wondering if it's going to rain tonight. Then I look over to my dog tucked into the riverbank. She raises her head to a distant rumble; I do the same. It's true, really. I didn't just say it to spike the conversation. Jesse *is* my guru, reminding me daily about the importance of being in the moment. Whenever I start getting too bogged down in my own abstractions, she's there to set me right. But society doesn't put much credence in the wisdom of dogs or rants of backwoods philosophers, so now what? Backpack and fly rod come in handy whenever the tension between me and my fellow man gets to be too much. These leisure tools help me get away, anyhow. But the wild itself is a constant reminder that I can't censor myself indefinitely about matters of ultimate concern. It's a paradox to be sure.

2

A gentle rain fell overnight as thunderstorms rolled through the region. Yesterday's heat has given way to morning coolness. Jesse is invigorated by it. She jumps to her feet and starts chasing her tail in an unexpected display of enthusiasm. I put an end to a long, lazy breakfast routine and start packing. My camp companions, slow to rise and get going, are now at it as well. A few minutes later they are back on the trail, headed north. Shortly thereafter, Jesse and I are southbound.

Today we're going as far as Cedar Lakes, about five miles away. The Northville/Lake Placid Trail climbs over the shoulder of Lamphere Ridge, then drops into a narrow valley. It's pretty easy going – road grade most of the way. All the same, the trail has a wilder feel to it now, twisting and turning through the trees, around rocks, over exposed roots and across muddy little bogs. Jesse's out front at first, but soon falls behind me. In trail-pounding mode now, a habit developed during my month-long trek on the Long Trail, I'm moving a bit too fast for her. So I stop and drop my pack when the trail reaches the valley stream. That gives Jesse time enough to slake her thirst. She wades into the middle of the stream. Here the Cedar River is a mountain brook: cold, clear, shallow, about ten yards wide. It has an amber hue to it as most Adirondack streams do, but is clean enough to hold trout. I consider breaking out my rod and testing its waters, but no, I'm in hiking mode now. So then, after sharing a handful of peanuts with Jesse, I return to trail pounding.

The trail climbs back up the Lamphere Ridge, even though my map shows it hugging the stream. Hmm, that's a serious discrepancy. I check my compass as a precaution before going any farther. Decades of backcountry travel have taught me never to completely trust trails. More than once, I've followed well-beaten paths into oblivion.

Around noon Jesse and I drag our feet into a clearing next to Cedar Lake, where a lean-to offers some shelter from a thin drizzle. Two slender, thirtyish women are hanging out at the lean-to. They have no overnight gear, though. This puzzles me. A ribbon of smoke coils from the fire pit – their way of keeping the bugs at bay. We chat a bit. I learn that they've just day hiked here using a trail from the east, after leaving their car near Pillsbury Mountain. That's surprising. My map shows that trailhead four miles farther east, at Perkins Clearing. That means Cedar Lake is more accessible than I thought. That means there will be other people here.

Another mile down the trail, I cross a footbridge between a shallow body of water called Beaver Pond and the much larger Cedar Lake. Just past the footbridge, a narrow path appears on the left. No sign indicating a shelter that direction, so I keep to the main trail. After a steady, quarter-mile climb, I realize my mistake and retrace my steps back to the unmarked path. Sure enough, there's a shelter a hundred yards down it, occupied by a couple middle-aged canoeists and their two sons. Not wanting to impose myself on them yet in no mood to continue hiking, I follow the narrowing footpath beyond the shelter, skirting the shoreline. About fifty yards away, I find an old fire circle on a patch of flat, open ground among the trees. This will do. I pitch my tarp beneath an old beech to make the place my own.

Completely exhausted, Jesse collapses onto the forest floor. She doesn't move for hours, not even when a bold chipmunk scurries through camp. Poor dog. I pushed her hard today. Pushed myself, too, it seems. There are several hot spots on my feet and one rather large blister on my right heel. Guess the insoles of my boots have broken down more than I thought. Oh well. After setting up camp, I join Jesse for a long, mid-afternoon nap.

An hour or so later, I awaken to the all-too-familiar sound of rustling leaves. Looking over, I spot that pesky chipmunk helping itself to the food bag that I've carelessly left on the ground. I order Jesse to chase the intruder out of camp, but she only stares at the chipmunk, then at me, as if to say she hasn't the energy for it. Exasperated, I fling a stick at our unwelcome guest. That spooks the critter for a while, but ten minutes later it's creeping back into camp again. Finally, I get up and hoist the food bag into the air about eight feet or so, using a cord slung over an overhanging tree branch. And that settles the matter.

Loons call out. I grab my fly rod and scramble down the steep bank to the water's edge to see what's going on. Jesse follows. Several loons bob along the choppy surface, about a quarter mile out. Cedar Lake is big by backcountry standards: several miles long and nearly a mile wide in places. Remarkably pristine. A few shelters dot its shoreline otherwise there are no manmade structures. Some canoeists are fishing in the middle of the lake – my next-door neighbors, I think. Aside from them, there's no one in sight. Nothing but Adirondack wildness for as far as the eye can see. Pillsbury Mountain rises a few miles beyond the opposite shore. What else? Lots of hemlocks, birches and maples along the rocky shoreline. Few cedars, despite the lake's name. Clouds gather around the mountain. A strong southerly wind gives the lake a gray chop. The loons don't seem to care.

Breaking out my rod, I ply the roily water for trout. Jesse watches from a sandy spot along the rocky shore. Slowly, almost without realizing it, I slip into a funk. The fish aren't biting but that's not the issue. I'm troubled by something else – by some vague longing, an indistinct hunger for god-only-knows-what. My mood defies the lake's beauty and serenity. I don't understand it. I'm so disturbed by the incongruity between my mood and the surrounding landscape that I quit fishing shortly after starting then go directly back to camp to fix dinner.

Our dinner routine has become rather elaborate recently. First I reconstitute dried milk, then mix Jesse's enzyme powder into it – a rather dubious substitute for her failing pancreas. While the enzymes are activating, I get my own meal going. Fifteen minutes later, I shove several different pills down Jesse's throat – a witches brew of antibiotics and steroids – then add a ration of dried dog food to the brownish, frothing milk. Jesse eats slowly but devours every kibble. She used to be as fussy as a cat about food. Not any more. The steroids make her ravenous. Afterward, she drifts to the edge of camp, finding a nice, soft place in the forest duff to rest. I start a fire and boil up water for ramen and tea. My small fire burns smokeless in the fading light. I check on Jesse every once in a while just to make sure she hasn't wandered into the darkening woods. Not that she would. She's a frail old dog and the forest has teeth, so she stays close to camp.

Twilight lingers. I think about my wife, Judy, and how much she would like this place. Judy loves clear, backcountry lakes and ponds. But I'm out here by myself right now and that's for the best. Married to me over a dozen years, she knows all too well how much I need solitary excursions into deep woods to maintain my sanity. Still, it gets harder and harder to be out here for extended periods of time without her. The last time I was on the Northville/Lake Placid Trail, she was with me. We enjoyed a lazy week in the woods just north of Duck Hole. Nothing remarkable happened on that trip and that's precisely what made it such a great outing. We spent more time lounging next to a mountain stream than anything else. Yeah, she would like it here. She and Jesse would spend an entire day just swimming about and watching loons, as they have before.

Twilight becomes darkness. My cup of tea is gone now and I've burned most of the wood gathered before dinner. But I'm still in a funk and not sure why. As the bright orange tongues of fire lick back the night, I search them for some insight into myself and the world at large. Nothing emerges from the flames. Patience, patience... Another day or two out here and the wild will draw it out of me, as it has before. It always does. That's the main reason I come out here, isn't it? Spiritual housecleaning. Time alone in the woods forces everything to the surface.

Big day tomorrow. I secure camp against rain while letting the fire burn down to cooling embers. I call in Jesse who's standing guard about ten yards out. I direct her to a nice cushy spot next to me beneath the tarp. We both need a good night's rest. Tomorrow we're headed for West Canada Lake, five miles farther down the trail. After two years of daydreaming about the place, I'll finally get to see it. Looking forward to that.

3

Wednesday, August 7th. Third day in the woods. I roll out of my warm, dry sleeping bag and into a cool, damp camp. A light rain has soaked everything. Fortunately, I had the foresight to cover a small pile of sticks with a piece of plastic before going to bed so starting a fire this morning isn't a problem. I pull down the food bag and start breakfast. Jesse wanders away for a quick pee, then drops onto a patch of grass next to the trail to watch the lake. Before the fire burns clean, I consider changing my hiking plans. During a brief encounter with a thru-hiker yesterday afternoon, I learned that several groups are camped at West Canada Lake. I vaguely recall passing a side-trail pointing northwest, about halfway between here and that first lean-to a mile back. Saw a makeshift sign at that trail junction, I think, with the words "Lost Pond" scrawled on it. Can't help but wonder what's up that way. Maybe it's time to leave the beaten path. Hmm. Will have to give the matter more thought later on.

After breakfast, as the campfire embers cool, I sip coffee while poring over my maps. It doesn't take long to find the trail connecting Cedar Lake to Lost Pond and to devise a rather circuitous route north/northeast, back towards Cedar Flow. Taking that route will shorten this outing by ten miles, making things a bit easier for Jesse. Would get me into wilder country, as well. But that would mean abandoning my trek to West Canada Lake. How important is it to reach that body of water? Not nearly as important as shaking off the funk that's been hounding me lately. I really need to spend some time alone in *deep* woods. Lost Pond looks like just the place to do that. It's out of the way, to be sure. Not much reason for anyone to go there. Might even get lucky and have it entirely to myself for a couple days. Wouldn't that be something. A shortened trek would mean that Jesse and I could hang out another day here at Cedar Lake, as well. She could certainly use the down time. Speaking of which… where'd she go?

Walking over to where Jesse had been resting, I look over the steep bank to find her lying in the sand next to the lake. I snuff out my fire, grab my rod and join my lazy dog. It's a calm, quiet, partly cloudy day. The lake's surface is still. No fly hatch. Not the best conditions for fly fishing, but I don't care. I cast my line repeatedly, letting my thoughts sink deep into the lake with my wet fly. Directly across the lake, several loons kick up a racket in a place appropriately called Noisey Inlet. Their haunting calls echo off Pillsbury Mountain. The clouds clinging to the mountain make it appear bigger than it really is. Canoeists floating in the middle of the lake are also trying to fish. Jesse catches a scent in the air. I can only guess what it is. And hours slip away effortlessly.

Late afternoon. I'd be hard-pressed to say what I've done today. Washed a few clothes, sketched, napped, walked over to the nearby Beaver Pond to check it out – what else? After swimming naked in the heat of the day, I stretched across a boulder to watch clouds drift past for a while. A wood duck stopped by for a visit, then a raven. Following Jesse's lead, I've been doing a lot of nothing. Radical deceleration. Can't say that I'm completely in tune with the wild, but I have slowed down enough to notice things I wouldn't have noticed before. Like the way the lake changes its mood during the course of the day, for instance, and how that changes me.

Early evening, I get serious about fishing. A few mayflies appeared on the water just as I was finishing dinner, so now I'm throwing a #18 Adams dry fly out there to float among them. The occasional surface splash gets me going. I pay close attention, keeping my line tight and watching the water intently. Soon enough, wild trout attack my offering. Several near misses, then I hook one. A short fight brings a nine-inch brook trout to the shore's rocky edge where it works itself loose. Close enough. Jesse and I both get a good look at it. I cast again. More flies hatch, more splashes, more action at the end of my line as the daylong breeze gives way to dusky stillness. Jesse wades chest-deep in the lake to do a little fishing of her own. At one point, she chases a fish that I've hooked into the shallows where my line wraps around a rock then snaps. I laugh then tie on another fly with some difficulty, holding it up to the sunset's afterglow. Now my fly is almost impossible to find floating in the dark, watery void. When finally the bats come out, the fish go into a feeding frenzy. But it's too dark to see anything at all. I'm done. I return to camp empty-handed yet happy to call it a day.

Thursday morning I'm awakened by the persistent knocking of a hungry woodpecker. Slept well last night, lulled into the land of dreams by a great horned owl. Down by the lake, I splash cold water into my face while listening to a solitary loon in Noisey Inlet. The sun peeks through the trees, then burns a hole in the clear blue sky just left of Pillsbury Mountain. A thin mist rises from the glassy lake. The day couldn't be any more promising. Jesse feels the same way I do, breaking into a big smile as she scans the lake and sniffs the air. We exchange knowing looks before returning to camp.

Jesse slips into play mode after breakfast, excitedly chasing her tail like a young pup. I take my time breaking camp, savoring the comfortable familiarity of the place. Lost Pond is only three miles north so there's no need to rush. All the same, I'm eager to hit the trail and get going. Forty-four hours is long enough to stay in one place. Both Jesse and I are in the mood to move.

I drop a handful of nuts near the campfire circle for that chipmunk bandit to enjoy then brush the ground with a spruce bough to give the site a less-beaten look. One last look around before hoisting the backpack to my shoulders and heading out. Jesse is already on the trail.

Backtracking half a mile, across the footbridge then turning away from Cedar Lake, I find the sketchy side trail that I'd largely ignored the day before yesterday. Sure enough, there's a sign at the trail junction with the words "Lost Pond" etched on it. The narrow path is barely worn yet well marked by yellow discs. Goodbye Northville/Lake Placid Trail, hello deep woods! I tap my walking stick against a birch tree a couple times for good luck then head north.

Deer tracks and a couple sets of boot prints – I'm not the first one to travel this way. Hope no one's camped at Lost Pond. If so, I'll keep going until I reach Little Moose Lake a bit farther north. I'm flexible. The thin layer of soil underfoot leads me to believe that very few people ever use this trail. Winding through the forest this way and that, it looks as if the person who blazed this trail became disoriented. Not a very direct path, that's for sure. But it's pleasant to walk all the same. The trail skirts the wetlands of Beaver Pond, that's the main thing. Then it rises out of the lowlands after crossing the pond's outlet and tags an abandoned logging road. Couldn't be easier walking, even though there's a steady uphill climb for half a mile. Sweating and a bit winded after cresting the shoulder of a small mountain, I stop to catch my breath. Jesse looks like she could use a little rest, too.

I study the surrounding forest while sucking down water and munching some trail mix. The tightly knit birches and spruces down by Beaver Pond are gone now. The surrounding woods are bright and airy. Mostly beeches. A good number of them have claw marks in their bark. Jesse sniffs a pile of fresh scat then knits her brows. "That's right," I respond with a laugh, "This is bear country." Jesse doesn't like it. I produce a couple dog biscuits to take her mind off the troubling discovery, but she clings to my side when we get going again. Sick old dog in the wild – yeah, she's a target all right. But I assure her with a neck rub that everything's going to be okay, that I won't abandon her.

What a beautiful stretch of wild forest! What a glorious day! And drifting slowly along the old woods road couldn't be any easier. Shafts of light break through the green canopy, illuminating the forest. The boot prints have disappeared for one reason or another so now these woods are all mine. Yessir, this is what it's all about. Glad I left the main trail. Can't wait to see Lost Pond. Will probably have it all to myself. Wonder if there are any trout in it. I beam a big smile at Jesse but she still looks worried. "For chrissakes, Jes, the bears aren't going to get you," I snap at her. Then I start humming a tune. Not going to let my worrisome dog spoil the moment.

4

When the trail suddenly descends after turning sharply to the east, I stop to check my map and compass. Something's not right. It's supposed to follow the contours westward for a while. Why are the yellow discs taking me some other direction? Either the trail has been rerouted recently or my map's wrong. Hmm. Not one to turn back and not in the mood to leave the trail just yet, I stay with the yellow markers. Guess I am trusting them now.

The trail drops fast, leveling out just before reaching a small wetland. Next thing I know, the trail markers are running across the top of a beaver dam. Is this some kind of joke? Blindly following the markers, I step gingerly across the tangle of sticks and grass, trying to keep my boots dry. Jesse has more trouble crossing the dam than I do, slipping into the muck a couple times. Somewhat relieved to reach the tall grass on the other side of the dam, I temporarily lose sight of the yellow discs. But they reappear once my feet tag high ground again. When the trail slips into a copse of shadowy conifers, markers become few and far between. I suspect that the narrow path underfoot wouldn't even exist if it weren't for deer. There's no indication that anyone else has come this way in a while.

After bearing right for a quarter mile, I come to a sign in the middle of nowhere: "Lost Pond .8 mile." An arrow on the sign points sharply to my right, leading me to believe that I'm walking in circles. A quick glance at my compass verifies this. Completely disoriented now, I follow the yellow markers as they weave in and out of the trees. What was once a track cutting through the dense forest is now a series of mud holes. Jesse follows, assuming that I know where I'm going. Shortly after losing the yellow discs, I catch a little light through the trees. Lost Pond, I presume. Appropriately named, that's for sure. I have only a vague idea where I am right now.

Stepping into the open, first thing I notice is that the pond is entirely surrounded by sphagnum moss. It's a shallow body of water in the middle of what would otherwise be a large bog. No easy access. I drop my pack and walk to the edge of the turf to test its stability. Jesse bounds ahead of me. "No!" I yell, but it's too late. Before the sound of my voice has stopped echoing through the surrounding hills, she's chest deep in muck. I lean over and grab Jesse by the collar as she scrambles back onto the turf. Great. Now the lower half of her body is covered with black mud. Swamp dog. How am I going to clean her up? I look around for a feeder stream but see nothing but timber and turf.

Just then the middle of the pond erupts. I look over to see a huge trout leap two feet into the air then splash back into the drink. Shock waves ripple across the water's surface, all the way to the distant beaver dam. The fly fisher in me stirs to action, but there's no wading across the pond's mucky bottom and from here I can't cast that far enough to be effective. Damn!

Lost Pond has an utterly wild, almost spooky feeling to it. I'd like to stay here and groove on it for a while but there's nowhere to camp. Nothing but sphagnum moss and thick black spruce in all directions. The sun is high in the sky now and the temperature is climbing. I'm thirsty. My bottles are nearly empty and there's no good water source at hand. The pond is the color of dark ale. Meanwhile, I've got a muck-covered dog to contend with. Fact is I can't stay here. I've got to find a relatively clean stream.

One last look at the remote pond, reminiscent of other wild places I've been, then I turn away. Now what? Whipping out my map, I study the contours and make an educated guess as to where I'm likely to find a trickle of clear water. More importantly, where am I and how do I get out of here? According to my map, I went through a trail junction about half a mile back. At that sign perhaps? Back there I should find a path connecting Lost Pond Trail to a woods road leading to Little Moose Lake. Surely I'll find some kind of feeder stream along the way. So then, without further hesitation, I shoulder my pack and get going. Swamp dog is right on my heels.

Backtracking to the "Lost Pond" sign is easy. Finding the connector trail isn't. After looking around a minute or two, I find the trail hidden behind the thick branches of a fallen hemlock. Not much of a trail, really, but the yellow disc that I spot on it assures me that it'll take me where I want to go. I step around the fallen hemlock then head down the trail. And there it is – a feeder stream! Putting my water filter to good use, I slake my thirst while filling both bottles. Then I clean up Jesse. But the ankle-deep rivulet clouds up right away. And a swarm of mosquitoes urges me to get going long before I can wash all the muck out of Jesse's fur.

Now then, to reach that woods road... After following the feeder stream another fifty-yards, the connector trail crosses it. But there's no semblance of a path on the other side. What just happened? I backtrack, look around, go this way and that, but there's no more trail. Jesse grows anxious, reacting to my indecision. She tries to lure me back the way we came. I tell her we're not doing that. She responds with whimpers, dancing back and forth. That sets me off. "Hey, I'm the one calling the shots here," I growl at her. Then I ponder my next move. There's only one thing to do, really. I shoot a compass bearing due north. If there's a woods road running east/west, as shown on my map, we'll soon run into it. "Let's go!" I shout with all the authority I can muster, pressing into the trackless forest. Jesse follows obediently.

We bushwhack less than a hundred yards before stepping onto the sketchy woods road. Jesse gives me that I-wasn't-really-worried look. Yeah, right. Turning eastward, we soon stumble into an old, rusty signpost half-hidden by brush. It points in the general direction of Lost Pond. I drop my pack at the base of the sign and tramp down an overgrown trail until I reach the feeder stream where I'd been standing fifteen minutes earlier. Now it all makes sense. Back at the rusty sign, I whip out my map to finish orienting myself. Then I sit down to eat something. Lunch is a simple affair: trail mix, some crackers, beef jerky. Jesse gets a couple biscuits and we're both happy.

Slowly meandering eastward along the woods road, it's clear that no one has traveled this way in a long, long time. Fallen trees block the track every thirty or forty yards. Saplings grow waist high in the middle of the road. The trail underfoot is a deer path now, weaving through thickening brush. Every once in a while, I spot a snowmobile trail marker. That convinces me that this track could be opened again someday. But right now, it's forgotten.

Mid-afternoon. After daydreaming along the abandoned woods road for an hour or so, I spot an opening through the trees to my left. Can it be? Sure enough, there's a beaver pond fifty yards south the woods road, about a hundred feet below us. It's small, deep and still. No brush around it. What a beauty! I drop my pack and take a long break to admire the gem before me.

Being a backwoods fisherman, I love little surprises like this. Located at the head of a mountain stream that eventually pours into Cedar River, this pond could be holding trout. If so, I could be the first person to fish it. Looks like there's a good access to its deepest water, just above the dam. Hmm. Should I keep going until I reach Little Moose Lake or stay here for the night and fish the pond at dusk? Could be brook trout heaven. I've stumbled into beaver ponds like this before and pulled nine-inchers from them all day long. Or it could be a dud. What day is this? Thursday. That means I still have enough food for three or four more days. Why not stay here a while?

Late afternoon, early evening. I've set up camp in the middle of the woods road, much to the dismay of any deer that might come along tonight. A flat, roomy spot surrounded by hardwoods, it feels like home immediately after I pitch the tarp and fashion a fire circle. The pond is in clear view. A beaver swims about the pond as I gather wood. Unhappy about Jesse and me being here, he slaps his tail against the water. Jesse is startled by it. We walk down to the pond's edge to fill a water bladder a bit later. The beaver slaps his tail one more time as he dives for cover.

Using my camp stove, I boil up the brackish water to purify it. Don't trust my filter to do the job. The process goes quickly enough. Afterward, dinner is an expedient affair – more for Jesse's benefit than mine. I eat whatever doesn't need to be cooked. Jesse's bowl is the only thing that requires washing. Soon enough, dinner's over and camp is all squared away. With an hour or two of daylight left, I grab my rod and whistle for Jesse to follow me. She's surprised by this, thinking that we've settled in for the night. But she's on her feet in a heartbeat.

Reaching that patch of open ground next to the beaver dam is harder than I thought it would be. A thick stand of black spruce blocks direct access, so I'm forced to sweep widely to the left, through a small wet meadow just below of the pond. Naturally the meadow is crisscrossed by beaver channels – in anticipation of even newer ponds. I skip across a fallen log stretching over the largest channel. Jesse follows but her unsteady hind legs slip away beneath her, putting her chest-deep in muck for the second time today. She yelps, unable to escape the muck. I reach over and grab her by the fur to haul her free. Shaken by this, she follows me to the open ground with some reluctance. I coax her into a nice soft spot next to the pond to rest. She lies down with a heavy sigh.

Clouds of mayflies hatch shortly after the sun sinks into the trees. No fish rise but it's a glorious thing to behold such a strong hatch of aquatic insects. I cast my artificial fly among the living ones, projecting myself into the rhythm of things. This profusion of aquatic life, far away from the hubbub of humanity, queues me to a cycle that's been turning for eons. My thoughts swim in the wonder and mystery of it all. Now I'm fishing more for perspective than anything else. Mesmerized by the silence and stillness of the pond, I stop waving my rod and simply watch things unfold around me. Eventually, a dragonfly buzzes my head, drawing me out of my reverie. Daylight has become twilight already. Better get back to camp.

After a quick wash in the brackish pond, I declare Jesse clean again. Then we head out. I fight my way through the dense spruce – hard going for me but easy on my four-legged companion who's low to the ground. A few cuts and scrapes later, I pop into the roomy hardwoods and scramble uphill. Jesse collapses into a clump of grass as soon as we reach camp. She's completely spent. It's been a long, rough day for her. I rub her neck, promising that tomorrow will be easier. She doesn't respond. Darkness comes fast. I strike a match, then hold it to the strips of birch bark piled inside the fire circle. Time for a little campfire meditation.

5

A small fire burns brightly in the circle of rocks before me. Its cheery orange flames provide good company as darkness descends. I've been here before – on my own in wild country with only a rough idea where I am. As always, the accompanying emotions are both oppressive and liberating. It's always a bit burdensome to be completely alone with one's thoughts in deep woods. But never is my head more clear than at times like these.

Jesse moves away from the fire, taking up guard duty at the edge of camp. With her back to me, she watches and listens for any kind of activity. A small creature rustles across the forest floor; a larger one bangs around the meadow below the beaver pond; mosquitoes whine. That's all that I can hear, anyhow, above the crackle of the campfire. The rest is deep forest silence, which torments ears accustomed to hearing so much more. Without realizing it at first, my mind invents cricket sounds to fill the void. Does Jesse do the same or is she more in tune with reality? I hear a slight humming sound in the distance, or at least *think* I hear something like that. It's the collective buzz of civilization, the dull echo of distant machinery. Or perhaps it's nothing at all.

Patches of deep blue sky filter through a web of branches directly overhead – the last glimmer of daylight. A green stick hisses then snaps loudly in the campfire. A wood thrush sings its melodious, flutelike song, reminding me of another place and time. Suddenly I'm twenty-four years old again, taking lunch somewhere in Oregon's Cascade Mountains. I remember a thrush landing on a tree branch not six feet away, serenading me. Never before had I ventured so deep into such a large wilderness area. Never before had I heard anything so beautiful. Later on that day, I left the beaten path in search of true wilderness. Twenty-odd years later, here I am doing much the same. What began as an impulse has become a lifelong habit.

Lost Pond was something of a disappointment. It wasn't the clear water haven I'd hoped it would be. But this camp next to a relatively new beaver pond is a good consolation prize. So it goes when you leave the beaten path. Roll with the punches; be ready to be surprised. That's what I like most about backcountry travel, I suppose. It forces me to be flexible, to abandon my linear way of thinking. It forces me to deal more directly with the world. It makes my thoughts less abstract. It makes my heart more receptive to *otherness*. But all these years of wandering and wondering – to what end? Today I've danced the spirit of the wild, no doubt about that. But am I any wiser for it? The wood thrush sings its forest hymn one last time this evening. I hear the earth rejoicing in that song, yet never have I felt such profound sadness. Perhaps this is only the passage of time leaving its mark on me. Or maybe I'm just tired. The fire dwindles until a skeleton of charred sticks collapses into a heap of glowing embers. I snuff out the remnants then go to bed.

First light. I awaken to the sound of breaking branches down by the beaver pond. Jesse hears it, too. A moment ago, I was playing with my grandkids in the land of dreams. Now I listen intently for the distinct rustle of a deer moving swiftly through the forest. There it is! Then silence. A wood thrush sings loud and clear. Perhaps it's the same one that I heard last night. It reminds me of something Henry David Thoreau once wrote: "The thrush alone declares the immortal wealth and vigor that is in the forest..." That puts a smile on my face as I crawl from bed. But Thoreau isn't my guru – not any more. He never was, really. Guys like me don't have gurus. We have only an insatiable appetite for knowledge and the company of furry companions on hair-shirt adventures. Yeah, I've read Henry's journals. And I know enough about the man to know the limits of his vision. So to hell with him and gurus in general. As both a woods wanderer and wonderer, I'm on my own now. I always have been, really. Just me and wild nature... and my ever-present dog, who's reminding me that it's time to drop the food bag and get the day going.

While fixing breakfast, I can't help but laugh. Henry would have approved of my fierce individualism, wouldn't he? Yeah, marching to the beat of a different drummer and all that. I say "To hell with you, Henry," and he responds with ghostly applause. It's ironic, actually. By dismissing that 19th Century iconoclast, I embrace him.

Just then it all makes sense: the funk, my writer's angst, my being here in deep woods, last night's dream, everything. Each life is but a lens – just one more way of seeing things. The suddenly I realize that it's not all about me, it's about whatever bit of insight I can contribute to humankind's ongoing spiritual adventure. Someday my perspective might be of use to others, perhaps to my grandchildren or my great grandchildren. *Someone* has to point the way to the wild – why not me? I brood that no one cares about what I scribble down, but how the hell do I know what'll resonate with people a hundred years from now? It's not about me – that's the main thing. I'm just a tool that wild nature uses. I'm just a set of ears to hear the wood thrush's song, and a pen to record it. That's all.

Where to begin? How does one speak for the wild? A single tear burns down my cheek as I look around me at the unspeakable beauty and power of the surrounding forest, feeling the presence of God as the sun rises slowly over the silent pond. There are no words for it, really. The wild is its own reason for being. It has its own agenda. So does Jesse. She comes over to drool all over me, wondering what the holdup is. "I'm getting to it," I grumble, pushing her away. Now then . . . where did I put her pills?

"C'mon, Jes!" I shout after shouldering my pack, tramping eastward along the overgrown woods road. She sprints ahead of me in a sudden burst of energy. It's a brand new day and we're both feeling frisky. Temps in the 60s and nothing but blue sky overhead. It's a great day to be in the woods.

We follow a set of fresh deer tracks through a small wetland then bear left as the narrow trail underfoot sweeps around Manbury Mountain. We're headed for Little Moose Lake, which I hope isn't overrun with people. According to my map, there's an unimproved dirt road skirting the northern rim of that lake. But my map is probably ten years old. The lake could be a resort by now. Or the road around it might be as forgotten as the trace I'm following. Won't know until I get there. Will reach it before noon. Hmm. With that thought, I cut my pace. No sense in racing out of the woods.

Eureka! I thought there might be a rivulet or two running off the mountain and sure enough, here's a nice one. The abandoned woods road crosses a stream small enough to jump across. Jesse immediately laps up the cold clear water. I drop my pack and extract a water filter from it. Then I fill both my bottles while sitting cross-legged on a patch of cool moss next to the stream. Mosquitoes hover over the nearby pool, more interested in seeking shelter from the rising heat than extracting blood from me. Jesse wades into another pool. I take advantage of the situation and wash her off a bit more. Then I splash cold water into my face. Didn't realize what a hardship last night's relatively dry camp was until now. Eighteen hours without running water – totally uncalled for.

The hike becomes a meander. No rush at all. Just beyond two posts where a gate once stood, the woods road becomes even harder to follow, splintering into divergent paths at overgrown logging yards. "Private Land," a sign warns in the middle of nowhere. I bear right as the trail forks one last time, choosing the path that veers downhill. I check my compass but it's all guesswork now. Reading the contours, I surmise that Little Moose Lake should crop up soon. A sketchy path quickly becomes a worn jeep trail entering bottomland thick with alders and willows. And sure enough, the lake pops into view as I cross the small wooden bridge over its outlet stream. To my great surprise, there's a cabin on a rocky outcrop about halfway up the lake. There's also a dirt road on the other side of the bridge. It's narrow but well maintained. And thus my excursion into deep woods ends, just like that.

6

Turning right onto the improved dirt road, I commence a long walk eastward. Presumably, the road follows the northern shoreline of Little Moose Lake, but there's no lake in sight and the unbroken row of "No Trespassing" signs nailed to trees on my right prevents me from going through the trees for a quick look. The owner of that cabin jealously guards his/her privacy. Whatever. The sooner I get back into the woods, the better.

A hot, midday sun shines directly overhead as Jesse and I tramp down the exposed corridor. The dusty road is awash in eye-squinting light. We take a water break in the shade once we're beyond the inhospitable signs, but are soon back on the move and puffing again.

My map shows a jeep track extending southward from the road a quarter mile to the northeastern corner of the lake. In my mind's eye, there's a primitive boat-launch at the end of that track with a nice place to camp nearby. Turning right onto a partially overgrown track, I pursue this daydream, hoping to reach the lake. No such luck. The track underfoot diminishes to a game trail on the other side of a small meadow then slowly fades into open woods. Both Jesse and I sense that we're getting closer to water as the terrain slopes gently downward, but we turn around after ten minutes of bushwhacking. Once again, there seems to be a discrepancy between my map and reality.

Back on the dirt road, I soon hear a trickle of running water. A quick thrash through some high grass reveals a rivulet small enough to step across. Finding cool, clear water in a foot-deep pool, I drop my pack and pump both water bottles full. Jesse drinks her fill, of course. Then we're back on the dusty road again, headed southeast. When the road turns sharply north, I spot a rusty yellow gate blocking a woods road pointing due east. Hmm. Is this the track heading back to the Northville/Lake Placid Trail? After checking my compass, I start down it.

Once again, deer tracks thread through chest-high brush, weaving back and forth along the remnants of a woods road, dodging downed trees. It's the mere suggestion of a trail. After crossing a stream, I'm convinced that I'm going the right way. If things go well, I'll soon be standing on a bona fide trail again.

Worse case scenario: the track underfoot will drop into that wetland barely visible through the trees to the south. If that happens, I'll keep to high ground.

Jesse gets all excited when finally we step back onto the Northville/Lake Placid Trail, thus completing our sixteen-mile loop. After sniffing around a bit, she smiles. So do I. For the first time since yesterday morning, I know *exactly* where I am. Quick lunch break, then we head north along the well-beaten path. The hike is so easy that I'm soon paying more attention to wildflowers than anything else. Indian pipe, closed gentian and white wood asters line the trail. It's late summer in the North Woods. Soon the fringes of hobblebush leaves will rust and a hint of autumn will be in the air.

A half-hour of steady hiking is all it takes to reach a high-use campsite on the reedy shores of Cedar Flow. Jesse knows that the truck is parked a mile and a half farther north so she's surprised when I start setting up camp. She thinks our trek is over, but I'm not ready to go home just yet. Why not stay here a day or two?

Puttering around camp like an old man, it's late evening before I have everything squared away: tarp pitched, wood gathered, food bag slung and Jesse cleaned up. I spend an inordinate amount of time picking up trash and tidying up the fire pit. Dinner is an expedient affair – a dehydrated meal and a few handfuls of trail mix. At dusk I build a bigger fire than necessary, burning up charred pieces of wood scattered about the area. Jesse goes to bed early.

Morning, day six. A woodpecker is hard at work directly overhead; a loon calls from the waterway. I slept well last night despite a midnight chill. The sun is high in the sky over Cedar Flow before I commence my breakfast ritual. Must've been more tired than I thought. Jesse looks exhausted. Good thing we're not going anywhere today.

After Jesse devours her breakfast, I give her a second helping. I do not do this lightly. It cuts into our limited food supply, meaning that we'll have to leave the woods tomorrow. But this trip's over for the most part. I have several blisters on my feet and Jesse is at the limit of her endurance. I've pushed her long enough.

A steady stream of hikers tramp up and down the nearby trail. A few stop to chat while I putter around camp doing a lot of nothing. One thru-hiker shows off a homemade stove. A father/son team takes a much-needed break, trading stories with me. But most of the day it's just Jesse and me along the shores of Cedar Flow, watching a golden eagle soaring over the water, listening to loons, taking in the expansive view.

Early evening, I join a blue heron wading amid the reeds, fishing for dace. Standing thigh-deep in water, I catch and release a dozen of those tiny fish. It's a goofy pleasure, tossing my fly among live ones only to have baitfish suck it down. I don't care. The subtle change of evening light and the sensation of mud oozing between my toes is reason enough to stand here. Jesse watches from a comfy tuft of grass on the edge of shore, drifting in an out of consciousness. She couldn't look any more content.

At dusk Jesse goes crazy on me, pacing back and forth along the trail as I start a fire. She's had enough of the wild and wants to leave right now. I tell her we'll hike out tomorrow, but she's not listening. Twice she disappears from view, heading down the trail on her own. I end up tying her to a tree in the middle of camp. Catching her silhouette in the campfire light a bit later on, I can see how uneasy she is. Rowdy young men camped half a mile south are making a lot of noise. Maybe that's what's bothering her. I unleash her and she clings to my side. I cut my fire gazing short, knowing that Jesse wants to settle in for the night. It has come to this.

Down by the water, cleaning up before going to bed, I gaze up at the Milky Way stretching across the black canopy. I marvel at the immensity of space and our place in it. I sit on a rock for a while, drawing Jesse closer. A shooting star streaks across the night sky. Another one follows a short while later. I try to make a wish but nothing comes to mind. I rub my dog behind the ears, instead. What was it that had me so bent out of shape a week ago? It doesn't matter any more.

Sunday, seventh day out here. Leaving wild country is always tough when foul weather isn't nipping at your heels. Today couldn't be more pleasant, with temps in the 60s and plenty of sunshine brightening the forest. I linger in camp as long as possible but am back on the trail by late morning. The hike goes fast. We're out of the woods before noon. I wipe a week's worth of cobwebs away from my truck before firing it up. Jesse is all smiles as she sits on the passenger's side, head out the window. A couple miles down the road, I stick my head out the window, as well, for a taste of breezy happiness. Yeah, it has come to this: the needs and desires of man and dog blurring. For the past five and a half years, Jesse has been my guru, helping me wrestle all my abstractions into perspective. She's been a good companion in that regard. But we've just finished our last big outing together and it won't be long before I have to put her down. It'll be hard returning to the woods without her.

Sampling the Real

Both Richard and I are excited by the prospect of a three-day trek in Adirondack backcountry and our rapid pace reflects that. We have finally broken free from busy lives in the lowlands and everything we need is in the packs on our backs. We hike hard and fast around Putnam Pond and down the Grizzlie Ocean Trail, burning up the first mile in less than a half hour. Even after our first water break, we are still tightly wound and chattering nonstop. Two miles later, deep into the Pharaoh Lake Wilderness, we are still hiking strong. The midsummer heat has us both sweating profusely. No matter. We're happy to be here. And before we know it, the afternoon's five-mile hike is over.

Pharaoh Lake comes as something of a surprise. It's bigger than expected, nearly a mile across and well over a mile long. There's no indication that anyone else is here, even though our map shows a half dozen shelters and campsites around the lake. We drop our packs in front of a relatively new shelter then walk to the edge of a rocky outcrop for a better view. Richard scans the undeveloped shoreline with an intensity that suggests disbelief. He hasn't spent a great deal of time in backcountry. I don't think he's ever seen a place quite as wild as this. Either that or it's been a long time since he has. "Beautiful, isn't it?" I say. Richard nods his head. I nestle into a depression in the rock, munching trail mix, leaving him to his own thoughts for a while. Richard spots a loon and calls to it, but the loon doesn't answer back.

The deer flies that dogged us during the day's short hike continue to harass us as we fix dinner. In the heat of the afternoon, I told Richard that they would go away once evening came. Unfortunately, they haven't. I make a game out of swatting deer flies, then tossing them into the lake. The water near shore boils as a school of small fish rise to my offerings. Richard is somewhat amused by this. "Feeding your minions?" he asks as I swipe a fly from the air.

"Yes, I am," I respond, "And thoroughly enjoying it."

After dinner, our attention shifts from the broad lake to a fire in the pit right in front of the shelter. Darkness descends slowly. I hand Richard a copy of my latest book, printed only three days ago. I strip pages from a second copy and feed them to the flames. Richard wonders why I'm doing this. "It's something I do every time I publish a book," I say, but that's not much of an explanation. So I tell him how this small sacrifice to the wild humbles me, how seeing my words turned to ashes helps keep things in perspective. Richard doesn't quite understand my reasoning but he respects the sentiment behind it. He senses that there's something out here worth taking seriously, anyhow.

The wild is closing in around us, or is it the real? Richard and I discuss this matter while tossing sticks on the fire, smoking cigars and sipping Sambuca

– a licorice-flavored liqueur. It isn't an easy subject to broach. "Reality is brought to mind by the inadequacy of any statement of it," the poet William Bronk once said, and that's precisely what we're experiencing right now. Water laps quietly against the shoreline. Bullfrogs croak in the darkness. An owl hoots as the fire crackles and then, after a long silence, that solitary loon cries out. We grope for words. We mouth canned phrases, platitudes and clichés until finally we give up trying to verbalize it. Then we go to bed. During the course of the night, the wild speaks for itself.

Daybreak. We're out of bed in a flash. I'm achy from the previous day's hike and just a little stuffed up from the smoke and alcohol, but a cup of strong coffee gets me going. Richard is relaxed yet ready for the big day ahead. By the time we finish eating breakfast, I'm as ready as he is. So we break camp and go.

   "Looks like we're going to get some heavy weather today," I tell Richard after reading the sky. The humidity is quite high already. We hike around the southern tip of Pharaoh Lake and, sure enough, run into drizzle before reaching the foot of Pharaoh Mountain. Halfway up the mountain, the drizzle thickens to steady rain. "This is good," I report rather cheerfully, "The rain'll keep the deer flies down." Taking my extensive backcountry experience into account, Richard accepts this assessment without question. But I'm dead wrong. To my bitter amazement, the flies continue tormenting us even as the rain comes down in sheets. And the humidity does not abate. So we are bug-bitten *and* soaked to the skin before reaching the summit, along with being sweaty and exhausted. "I hope we get a view, at least," Richard says as we near the top, but right now the summit is in the clouds.

We stop on top long enough to catch our breath, slake our thirst and eat something, hoping that the fog will lift before a sweaty chill settles into our bones. No such luck. We have to go. "How come I end up in the clouds every time I climb a mountain with you?" Richard asks, recalling a similar hike a couple years earlier. I shrug my shoulders.

The trail, gradually descending the northern slope of Pharaoh Mountain, is much easier on our bodies than the steep ascent. I lose steam all the same. By the time we reach Glidden Marsh, I'm ready for an extended break.   There are flowers to look at here – Indian pipe, yarrow and shinleaf – and lots of ripe blueberries to pick and eat. I drop my pack and start munching. Richard isn't into it, though. "The bugs are pretty bad here," he says while brushing them away from his face.

"Just ignore them," I say, crouched in some low bushes, "Look at these berries! It's a bumper crop!" Richard's not impressed. He wants to get going. We've got a cloud of bugs around us now – black flies and mosquitoes as well as deer flies – so I can see his point. I shoulder my pack and we're on the move again.   But the cloud moves with us.

Turning eastward at the next trail junction, Richard and I begin a long discussion about where to camp for the night. We don't have a plan, really. We've been playing it by ear. I'm thinking we should camp at Horseshoe Pond not far ahead, but he'd like to go all the way to Rock Pond. We've already hiked eight or nine miles and Rock Pond is still several miles away. "That'll make this hike a forced march," I grumble. Richard says he'd like to leave the woods early tomorrow. He's got a lot of things to do when he gets home. This is news to me and I'm just a little upset that we're just now discussing it. But maybe I wasn't listening to him earlier. Or maybe the bugs are driving him crazy. Whatever. I suggest that we refill our water bottles at Lily Pond, halfway between his preferred destination and mine. Lily Pond could be a good place to camp. Richard agrees so off we go, swatting flies all the way.

There are seven young men camped at Lily Pond when we reach it. Worse yet, the access to the pond is shallow and muddy – guaranteed to plug my water filter. "Let's get out of here," I growl while turning around and storming away. Richard joins me back on the trail, not quite sure what just happened. He knows that I'm angry, though. "We're almost out of drinking water," I explain, "And that water source sucked. But there's a stream half a mile up the trail. We'll pump there."

Richard tries to lighten things up a bit as we walk, but I'm in a *really* pissy mood now. I brood over our misfortune until we reach the stream. There we pump water and drink our fill. It's a rather pleasant spot. A cool breeze blowing off the braided waterfall right in front of us keeps the bugs at bay. "I don't want to camp here," Richard says. Neither do I. Upon close inspection, the ground looks too damp and rocky. So we continue hiking.

We've tramped twelve miles by the time Rock Pond finally appears out of the forest. I'm dehydrated, overheated and exhausted. Richard isn't doing much better.   Half a mile around the pond, we find a relatively flat campsite on a spit of land. We drop our packs and call it home for the night. A quick dip in the pond washes away the dirt, sweat and misery of the day's hike. Richard sets up his tent while I fire up my camp stove. That's when I notice a rather ominous thunderhead, due west and coming our way.

As luck would have it, my camp stove craps out right before the water is hot enough to use. Couldn't be worse timing. I ask Richard to gather up as much wood as he can while I build a quick fire in the nearby pit. We need several cups of boiling water to transform our two bags of powder into warm meals. That means two pots of hot water, preferably boiling. Richard and I take turns blowing on the fire to keep it burning fast and hot. I produce one pot of hot water before the first raindrops fall. By the time the second pot reaches a boil, I'm soaked to the skin. I quickly retreat into the tent with the precious commodity. Richard isn't quite as wet, having taken shelter a couple minutes ahead of me. But he's wet enough.

Inside the tent, we change into dry clothes then gobble down the hot food. Outside, the downpour becomes a deluge. Lightning illuminates the tent fabric as twilight fades. We celebrate our victory over the elements, passing the flask back and forth until the Sambuca is gone. It's been one hell of a day. But right now we're well fed and relatively dry so life is good.

Tuesday morning, third day out. Richard and I awaken to predawn light and an eerie silence after a long night of thunderstorms. There are a few puddles of water in the corners of the tent, but our things are still dry for the most part. Richard hopes we can break camp before it rains again. I ponder this while snoozing. A few minutes later, a downpour commences. Richard bolts upright in his sleeping bag, rather perturbed by this sudden turn of events. I laugh uncontrollably. Once again, Mother Nature has confounded our plans. But the rain stops an hour later, just as we're finishing breakfast, so packing up isn't nearly as wet and muddy as it could have been.

A thin mist rolls over the glassy pond while I pump water for the three-mile hike ahead. Richard kills deer flies and tosses them to a surly-looking frog hunkered into a reedy corner of the pond. "Feeding your minion?" I ask. Then we both laugh.

The hike out goes too quickly for me. Not for Richard, though. Once we're back to the car, he says he has had enough of the wild for the time being. No wonder. The flies continue tormenting us even as we stuff our packs into the car. Our clothes stick to our bodies despite a drying sun. I must admit, it feels good to be bug-free and sinking deep into the soft seat of a car, enjoying a window breeze as we motor back to the lowlands. Usually a three-day outing isn't quite so rough.

Back at Richard's house, fatigue sets in as we separate our gear. I pile my stuff into the back of my old pickup, thinking that I'll need a large cup of coffee to get me home. While starting up my truck, I tell Richard not to work too hard. "It was kind of fun, wasn't it?" I add, fishing for some kind of positive note on which to end the trip.

"It was real," he says.

"Yes it was," I respond with a smile. Then I shift the truck into first gear and drive away.

An Exalted Dream

The misty, incredibly humid forest keeps me sweating despite cool morning air as I hike through the heart of Silver Lake Wilderness. Then comes a reprieve. The sky breaks open, illuminating a shallow stream near the trail. I squat down to refill two water bottles and slake my thirst. A shaft of sunlight glances off the water's surface, forcing me to look away. The warmth of it caresses my face. A songbird rejoices. Its unfamiliar melody lifts my spirits as water drips from my beard. Suddenly I am a denizen of this wet, green world full of mud, mushrooms and moss. I shoulder my heavy pack and continue up the trail.

A day and a half into my trek along the Northville/Placid Trail, I am just now awakening to wildness. It takes this long to get into the groove of things, to put behind me all the noise of the developed places. I notice a solitary white wildflower called Turtlehead while crossing greasy, half-rotten boards spanning a small bog. The dank smell of saturated humus fills the air as the forest slowly dries out. I step sideways to avoid crushing a red eft resting motionless in the middle of the path. One mile later, I drop my pack on the planked floor of Mud Lake Shelter to break for lunch.

The Northville/Placid Trail traverses four wilderness areas and several wild forests as it winds for a hundred and twenty-five miles from a trailhead just north of Great Sacandaga Lake all the way to Lake Placid. Avoiding the peaks, the NPT is a celebration of deep woods – the very thing that distinguishes the Adirondacks from every other heavily forested, mountainous playground east of the Mississippi. The North Maine Woods come close, but they are riddled with logging roads. Only in the Adirondacks can an Easterner escape the sights and sounds of civilization for days on end. The NPT revels in that wildness. That's why I chose to hike all of it in my fiftieth year.

Just beyond Mud Lake, I plant my trekking poles, sweating and grunting uphill until the trail crests a ridge. Then the forest shifts from dark, shadowy conifers to the bright, airy realm of birches, maples and beeches. I slip into reverie as the path underfoot eases ever so slowly down towards the Sacandaga River. Then I smile while recalling something Ralph Waldo Emerson once wrote in his journals: "A walk in the woods is only an exalted dream." How can any woods walker deny that? As much as I hate to admit it, I become something of a dreamy-eyed Romantic while hiking alone through the woods. The real and the ideal blur as I follow some windy path cutting through the green infinity, and I become joyful in a way that just isn't possible anywhere else.

In 1836, the same year that Ralph Waldo Emerson published a slender volume called *Nature*, a geology professor named Ebenezer Emmons climbed Mount

Marcy with the help of the backcountry guide, John Cheney. Shortly thereafter, Emmons returned to the Adirondacks with the newspaperman Charles Fenno Hoffman. Then word got out about the wonder and beauty of the wild country only a day's travel north of New York City. In the 1858, Emerson, James Russell Lowell, Louis Agassiz and seven other East Coast intellectuals retreated to a "philosophers camp" in the Adirondacks to sample the wild. By then people from all walks of life were heading for the hills.

Immediately following the Civil War, Reverend William H. H. Murray published his book, *Adventures in the Wilderness*. It became a bestseller, and soon urbanites weary of industrialization were flocking to the Adirondacks as a result. Meanwhile, as writers like Henry David Thoreau idealized the wild, George Perkins Marsh warned against clear-cutting the uplands. Marsh argued that they are vital sources of fresh water, and that deforestation threatens those sources. Verplanck Colvin, the man responsible for surveying much of the Adirondacks, embraced Marsh's argument, becoming an outspoken advocate for the protection of the wild. Because of his tireless lobbying, and the growing interest in nature among mainstream Americans, the New York State Legislature passed a law in 1885 creating the Catskill and Adirondack Forest Preserves. In the 1920s, the Adirondack Mountain Club was founded, and the first thing the club members did was blaze a footpath cutting through the latter. Today that path is known as the Northville/Placid Trail.

An exalted dream, no doubt, yet something more. I cross the Sacandaga River, pressing farther north. By the end of the day, I am exhausted, footsore, and interested only in flopping in a shelter to sleep. But the next day I am back on the trail again, completing my traverse of Silver Lakes Wilderness. Two days later, I am deep into West Canada Lakes Wilderness and wondering why more people aren't out here where bear and moose roam freely, and the call of loons echoes across pristine water. I don't just appreciate the wild – I revel in it. The wild feeds my soul. After several days on the trail, it becomes a part of me. The wild rises from deep within, strengthening a natural affinity with the elemental world. As a consequence, I become acutely aware of both my humanity and my animal self, and how they are inexorably entwined.

My trekking poles click against rocks as I charge up the trail, eager to see West Lake now only a couple miles away. Several years ago, I tried to reach West Lake from another direction, but it was too far away and I was short on time. Besides, I had developed a blister on one foot the size of a silver dollar. Now I have another blister in the same spot, but I don't care. West Lake is all I can think about. It has become the object of my desire precisely because it is so deep, so hard to reach. Nothing else matters, not even hiking the NPT in its entirety.

"How does Nature deify us with a few and cheap elements!" Emerson wrote in his Transcendentalist manifesto, *Nature*, "Give me health and a day, and I will make the pomp of emperors ridiculous." Spoken like a true woods walker. No doubt Thoreau endorsed that sentiment, as did every Romantic thinker of the mid-19th Century. Certainly I concur while tramping deeper into a forest left to its own devices for well over a hundred years.

Upon reaching West Lake Shelter, I douse a mound of hot ashes still smoldering in the fire pit. Then I gather up trash and half-empty liquor bottles scattered about the shelter. Clearly I'm not the only one out here, but my reverence for the wild isn't something shared by all. Whatever. I have not come here to judge. I unpack, making myself at home. I intend to rest up for a day or so before pressing farther north. The sky slowly turns crimson. Loons call out right before dusk. An owl hoots through the darkness afterward. I am delighted by it all. But it is the utter absence of sound at midnight that makes me sit up and take notice. Awakening to it, I am astounded. The lake is absolutely still. Moonlight washes over its glassy surface. And for a moment I can't tell whether I am awake or still asleep.

The next day I clean up, nap, bird-watch, what else? I do a lot of nothing. Deep in the wilderness and not rushing from one place to another, I slip into a mindset where *doing* seems rather silly – not nearly as important as *being*. The sun climbs high into the sky, creeps westward all afternoon, then sets. And I am completely immersed in the here and now. That is all. No grandiose notions about the world or myself, no abstractions. But the urge to get moving returns after a good night's sleep. Seventh day out, I gather up my things. Then I shoulder the heavy backpack, grab the trekking poles leaning against the shelter, and set forth. The trail beckons. It's time to explore that exalted dream a little bit more.

Mesmerized in Big Woods

West Canada Lakes Wilderness does not attract peak-baggers. It is not the place to go for panoramic vistas and exhilarating ascents. Nor are its trailheads located on state highways. Those who want to climb a big mountain should go to the High Peaks – that cluster of lofty summits at the very heart of the Adirondacks. That's the best place for a day hike or a quick overnighter. But a couple dozen miles southwest of the High Peaks, there's a roadless area so big that it rivals anything you'll find east of the Mississippi. Don't go in there unless your map and compass skills are up to snuff. Pack plenty of food if you do. Plan on staying in that wilderness several days if possible. Even then, you won't be able to see half of it.

When I set forth from the Benson trailhead last September, I had two distinct goals in mind: to hike the entire Northville/Placid Trail at one throw and, more importantly, to finally reach West Lake. Several years earlier, I had backpacked south out of Wakely Dam and had gone as far as Cedar Lakes before straying. Back then I was lured off the main trail by a mysterious place called Lost Pond. But this time there would be no digression. This time I was hiking north on the N/P Trail, determined to follow those blue trail markers all the way to Lake Placid. And West Lake was directly in my path.

It took two days to hike across the Silver Lake Wilderness. I traveled some twenty-five miles of winding trail, passing around a half dozen ponds and across as many bogs. That country had a big woods feeling to it, certainly. But even as I exited that wilderness, entering the town of Piseco, I knew that the woods directly ahead would be even bigger. I use the word "big" here to indicate distance from an improved road of any sort. In that regard, West Canada Lakes Wilderness is one of the biggest woods around.

At the Piseco post office, I picked up a small box of supplies. I had mailed it there, knowing that I'd need extra food in order to spend time at West Lake before continuing north. A full day's hike got me as far as Spruce Lake. I slept a night there then took off early the next morning, headed for the object of my desire. I reached South Lake by midday and West Lake less than an hour later. Yes, it was everything I'd hoped it would be: a clear lake in a wild and beautiful setting. Its rocky shoreline and the unnamed mountain rising from it were pleasant surprises, indeed.

Shortly after dropping my heavy pack at the foot of West Lake Lean-to #1, I stood along the water's edge, trying to grasp the remoteness of this place. I was sixteen miles beyond the road's end in Piseco, and there was another fifteen miles of trail between this spot and the next road north – a day-and-a-half hike either direction. In other words, I had arrived.

That evening, a pair of loons danced across the water as the sun dropped ever so slowly into distant trees. I cast my fly line as far from shore as possible while standing upon a large, flat rock protruding into the lake. The wind died away at dusk. The lake became a sheet of glass barely rippled by fish feeding at the surface. The wing-flap of a woodpecker passing directly overhead startled me, as did the hoot-hoot of a barred owl nearby. No, I didn't do battle as expected with the monster trout that supposedly live in West Lake, but that didn't seem to matter when a pink and gold sunset filled the sky. Once the afterglow faded, bats swooped low over the water, feeding on mosquitoes. A tree branch snapped somewhere across the lake and it sounded like it was going to fall on me. The silence that followed was deafening.

When I could no longer see my fly, I reeled in my line and called it a day. Then I stumbled through the darkness, back towards camp. While slipping through dense spruces, I felt something that I hadn't expected to feel. I felt strangely at home in a place I hadn't even seen before that afternoon. It was something I'd felt a couple times before – once in the Cascade Mountains of Oregon, then again in Alaska. It was as if the wild itself had taken me under its wing.

That night, I awoke to the haunting call of loons. Their cry echoed through the forest with all the force of raw nature behind it. And when they fell silent, there was nothing else to occupy my ears – nothing but the humming sound of blood coursing through my veins. The shock of this sudden, deep silence forced my eyes open. Then moonlight flooded into them.

A full moon had drifted high into the center of a cobalt sky and was illuminating both the lake and its surrounding hills. I was mesmerized by it, by the brilliant reflection of cosmic light and the utter lack of any movement or sound in the cold, still night. Times like these, I usually ponder life's big questions: How did the universe come to be? Why are we here? What's it all for? But this time I was completely disarmed. No thoughts whatsoever. Only that bright, white orb and my mind wiped clean by it. *Tabula rasa.* When finally an owl hooted, I snapped out of that trance, but not before the wild left its mark on me.

Too often I find myself in polite society, trying to explain why I feel this need to venture deep into big woods. Bagging peaks makes sense even to those who never do it. After all, a summit is a tangible goal with the guarantee of a good workout and the promise of great views. But why this endless tramping along wet, muddy, lowland trails, going deeper into green infinity, with the torment of black flies and mosquitoes all the way? Why suffer wind and rain, heat and cold, sweat and dehydration just to reach a pond or lake much like any other small body of water tucked into a sprawling, northern forest? "To seek out the wild," I say in my defense, but that's just me blowing smoke. After all, the word "wild" is as vague as the words "truth" and "love." Words like that can mean anything at all.

Big woods have one big thing to recommend them. They stand apart from our cultivated fields, gardens, city parks, farmhouses, suburbs and towns. In short, they are not of our making. Big woods are not tree farms. They are something else. They are places left as undeveloped as possible in a world where every piece of land has its purpose and price. So what, then, is the value of such places? I don't know how most people feel about it, but I go into big woods to humanize myself. As David Abram wrote in *The Spell of the Sensuous*, "We are human only in contact, in conviviality, with what is not human." Deep enough in big woods, I see nothing but wild nature. Except for the occasional plane passing overhead, I hear none of the mechanized sounds of civilization. And that helps me better understand who/what I am.

After a couple days at West Lake, I was ready to move on. I hiked strong and hard along the N/P Trail, past Cedar Lakes, past Cedar Flow, to Wakely Dam and beyond. Six days later, I was basking in that big woods feeling again. While camped along Cold River, somewhere deep in the High Peaks Wilderness, I was grooving with the wild just as I had at West Lake. But it wasn't quite the same. It was clear to me that the trail along Cold River gets a lot of use. By comparison, West Lake seemed more like the place that time forgot. Maybe that's because it's so hard to reach. When you're on foot, distance is everything.

About once a week, I drop what I'm doing, grab my pack and head for the hills. I usually hike into Vermont's Green Mountains, which is less than an hour away from my home here in the Champlain Valley. Every once in a while, I head for the High Peaks because I too like climbing big mountains. All this keeps me happy and healthy. But the next time I have a free week or more, I'm going back to West Canada Lakes Wilderness. My business there isn't finished. Maybe I'll catch a monster fish, maybe not. Either way, I'm sure to be mesmerized again. Big woods are good for that.

Loon Wisdom

The madness of civilization isn't apparent to those of us caught up in it. We read the morning paper, catch breaking news on TV, and speak with others about the vast array of evils running rampant in the world, but secretly we believe it doesn't affect us. We go about our daily affairs as if we live in a bubble. We put on our emotional armor in the morning then venture into traffic, fortified with a cup or two of coffee, alert yet confident that we can get to our workplace without mishap. And we usually do. But the madness takes root within us long before we punch a time clock or read the first email of the day. Only after countless days of this routine do we sense a growing uneasiness at the very core of our being. Something is wrong, terribly wrong, so we pick a well-defined target for all the pent-up unease, directing it at some family member, a co-worker, a client, the telephone company, or some abstract entity such as terrorists, liberals or authority, and everything makes sense again. Yet the madness remains firmly in place. Consequently, we fall victim to depression, confusion and road rage more often than any of us are willing to admit.

With all the desperation of a fugitive, I drive towards a big pocket of wild country one hundred and fifty miles from home. For weeks I have been hearing the call of loons in my head – a sure sign that this wilderness retreat is long overdue. For months I let circumstances keep me away from deep woods, so now I'm much worse for wear, as my white-knuckled grip on the steering wheel attests. During the last leg of a rapidly degrading dirt road, all I can think about is an unseen rock tearing the exhaust system from the belly of my car. That fear keeps me tightly wound until I reach the broad, flat parking lot at the end of the road and throw the automatic shift into park.

Minutes out of the car, I shoulder my backpack and amble up the trail with the help of a trusty, old walking stick. My dog, Matika, runs up and down the trail in a fit of unbridled exuberance. Although slower moving, I feel the same way. I venture deep into the sprawling forest. By the time I've worked up a good sweat, I've reached a sign announcing the West Canada Lakes Wilderness. This is one of the largest roadless areas east of the Mississippi. Located in the southwestern corner of New York's Adirondack Mountains, it is far enough away from the popular High Peaks Region to be overlooked by most hikers. I was here two years ago and am glad to be back.

Sampson Lake is seven miles from the trailhead and a dozen miles from the nearest paved road. I reach it late afternoon, drop my pack in front of the lean-to then hobble down to the shoreline for a look. The lake is beautifully wild, completely surrounded by forest, and eerily quiet as such places always are. Aside from the trampled, barren ground around the lean-to, there is no sign of human impact here. It's the perfect place to spend a few days, reconnecting with the wild, and that's exactly what I intend to do.

A loud cry breaks the silence. Matika's ears stand to attention as she scans the lake looking for the source of that sound. She doesn't know what to make of it. Neither do I at first. But when I hear the cry a second time, I figure it's a loon. A few minutes later, I locate the bird with my binoculars to verify this. Has it been so long since the last time I was in the wild that I don't recognize the loon's less familiar songs? Yes it has. But the boisterous call that the bird belts out a short while later is unmistakable. It is the sound of wildness itself, welcoming me back. And it feels good to be back. When the loon falls silent, I listen to a fire crackling and my own breathing well into evening, until my exhausted dog's snoring convinces me that it's time for bed.

It's all too easy to badmouth civilization while sitting before a campfire, deep in a wilderness area. Clearly I'm not the only one who does this. Gary Snyder had me convinced that "good, wild, sacred" was a credo I could embrace until he let loose his own fireside rant about humankind. "Civilization itself is ego gone to seed," he wrote in *The Practice of the Wild*, "And institutionalized in the form of the State." That rather misanthropic remark clung to me like a bur. I kept it close to my heart for many years, until I realized that it's patently untrue.

Civilization is human organization. We organize in order to make our lives better. Civilization is humankind addressing the myriad challenges posed by nature.   Snyder's bold statement smacks of anarchism, and like every "ism" – religious, philosophical or political – the wild refutes it.   The wild refutes all sweeping statements about human nature.   The wild has no agenda, takes no sides, supports no particular worldview.   Yet there exists a tension, no doubt, between civilization and the wild, between the human and everything else.   That much cannot be denied.

The madness of civilization is the truth of the world distorted to one end or another.   It is the source of all the confusion that we experience when we try to separate what is artificial from what is real.   As human beings, we are creatures of the abstract.   We prevail in this world by virtue of our cognitive powers, by sheer force of our imaginations, by our ability to think things then make them happen.   Civilization is the sum total of all our efforts to make the world work for us.   It is the human imposed upon nature with great success.   But the power of this abstraction comes at a price.   Not all our thoughts are good ones; not all our dreams can be turned into realities.   The unrealities left over from productive thought take root deep within us.   Because of these unrealities, there is madness in all of us, in all our priests, philosophers, scientists, artists, teachers and lawmakers.   There is madness in the end product, in civilization itself.   Consider the last time you set your clock back or forward an hour.   Did that action actually change nature?   Can a decree made by the State have any real impact upon the rising of the sun?   No.   Only our perceptions change – the way we do business with each other.   That is all.

Second day at Sampson Lake, a steady rain soaks me and the surrounding forest. Matika and I stay close to the shelter most of the day, venturing out for one long walk to nowhere and a few short trips down to the shoreline. I spot two loons floating about the grey, windswept lake – one female, the other male. They take turns calling out during the long, wet afternoon, breaking the quiet. I listen to them the same way I have always listened to loons: jolted into the here/now by their sudden wild laughter, then mesmerized by the echo of their cries diminishing to absolute silence. Then I listen to the silence itself, as if the truth of the world could be mine if I listened intently enough. Perhaps that is the purpose of the loon's manic call. Perhaps they flirt with the unspeakable, calling out loudly just to emphasize the nothingness that follows. Or perhaps they enjoy teasing us with the false promise of wisdom. Hard to say.

Wild nature is the truth of the world that words cannot touch, but this fact isn't very satisfying to those of us who call ourselves philosophers. So we ask ourselves "What is truth?" during outbreaks of rationalism, hoping to get to the bottom of things. We pose this question and a vast array of theories leap forth, until finally some smart aleck asserts that the truth is unknowable. Now what? Give that guy a cup of hemlock to drink then continue the argument. We have empires to build, civilizations to create, and dreams to fulfill. After all, we are *Homo sapiens sapiens* and we can do anything!

The French philosopher Blaise Pascal once said: "The eternal silence of these infinite spaces fills me with dread." Every time I stare deep into the night sky, I feel much the same way. And the boastful claims of empire builders roll off my shoulders like rainwater. Without uttering a sound, the universe undercuts all our magnificent abstractions. On the grandest scale, wild nature exceeds imagination. It is wilder than our wildest dreams. How can we comprehend it? Where are the words to describe what is real? Lakes we can dry up, forests we can cut down, and mountains we can move, but that's all child's play compared to the swirl of galaxies. Dread, yes, that's exactly what we feel when we stand face-to-face with cosmic reality. What little truth we possess begins and ends with that dread. We are confounded by our own abstractions, by our inability to see things as they simply are. And the loons are laughing.

Early in the morning on my third day at Sampson Lake, a loon calls out causing tears to well in the corners of my eyes. Suddenly I hear the voice of God in the loon's mad laughter. Suddenly I see myself for what I really am. No doubt tears flowed just as easily from Adam's eyes when he found himself cast out of Eden. Existential tears – the tears of a fully cognizant, self-aware creature escaping abstraction just long enough to see the world as a loon sees it. With my armor falling away and the wild exploding my preconceptions with all the force of a meteorite shower striking the earth, my abstract thoughts are reduced to raw emotion. Then silence reins. But it is only a fleeting moment of insight. Soon enough I am the same old abstract thinker I've always been. After all, I'm only human.

Matika doesn't relate to my tears. Even though she's utterly domesticated, her sympathies run more towards the wild. Resting comfortably on the ground, she listens to the loon and draws no conclusions. She'd chase down that bird given half a chance, clench her teeth around its feathered body, and maybe even make a meal out of it. Matika's never been a big one for entertaining abstractions. Yeah, she's perfectly happy leaving such matters to me.

Civilization is only what we make of it. If civilization has gone mad, it is only because we stubbornly cling to distorted versions of what is. The fix is simple: find a place in our lives for the wild as well as civilization; find a way to harmonize the two. This is easier said than done, of course, for we are abstract thinkers by nature and love our dreams as much as reality. Perhaps even more. But we can rise to this challenge if we want. After all, we are *sapient* creatures, and that's a quality that has brought us a long way during the past ten thousand years.

The Great Wild Silence

At West Lake there are no trucks or cars roaring in the distance, no train whistles, nothing to suggest the bustling world beyond the trees but a crosshatch of contrails left by jets in the sky above. The only structure standing next to the lake is a hiker's shelter. The nearest road of any sort is six miles away as the bird flies. The lake lies in the middle of West Canada Lakes Wilderness – the largest roadless area in the Adirondacks. It's a place where one can walk for days without encountering anything but the wild. And that's precisely why I wanted to go there.

I found West Lake while poring over topographical maps, looking for a blank spot to satisfy the wild urges awakened by my sojourn in the Alaskan bush many years earlier. I first attempted to reach the lake in 2002 by hiking south along the Northville/Placid Trail. I accessed that trail a few miles beyond Wakely Dam. I set aside seven days to reach the lake, hang out there for a while, and get back to my truck. On the third day I strayed. I left the NPT at Cedar Lakes, following an inviting, narrow path that took me to another place deep in the woods called Lost Pond. That digression reaped great rewards yet left me longing for the original object of my desire. Years would pass before I'd get another shot at it.

In 2006 I thru-hiked the Northville/Placid Trail from south to north. A day and a half out of a little town called Piseco, I finally reached West Lake. It was a warm, breezy afternoon in the end of summer. I had the place all to myself. No other people, that is. I shared the lake with wild creatures only – a couple loons, a few songbirds, and some ducks minding their own business. After settling into the shelter, I grabbed my fly rod and rock-hopped into the lake as far as I could go beyond the shoreline without getting my feet wet. Then I rolled out my line, dropping an artificial fly among the real ones rising to the lake's rippling surface. Wild trout were taking their evening meal as the sun dipped below distant trees. The sky turned crimson. The lake became glass. Suddenly the world was incredibly silent and still. And it stayed that way long after I returned to camp and went to bed.

In the middle of the night I awoke to the sound of my own breathing. I opened my eyes to see the moon shining high in the sky over the lake. The wild world around me was just as quiet as it had been at dusk. It was so quiet, so still that I could barely comprehend what was happening. Or perhaps I should say, what was not happening. I wanted to shout something to break the spell, but no utterance spilled from my gaping mouth. Instead the silence swallowed me whole, making me aware of something greater than myself. In her book *Holy the Firm* Annie Dillard wrote: "We wake, if ever we wake, to the silence of God." Clearly she too had experienced that awakening somewhere in the wild. It is hard to imagine it taking place anywhere else.

What is it that we escape when we venture into deep woods? More importantly, what is it that we seek there? Some 19th Century American thinkers considered the wild a remedy that could sooth souls sickened by a brand new phenomenon called industrialization. "We need the tonic of wildness," Henry David Thoreau asserted in his book, *Walden*. "The clearest way into the Universe is through a forest wilderness," John Muir added a few years later, expanding upon the theme. The many benefits of civilization should not be underestimated, nor should they be taken for granted. Yet something else has happened to us during the past century or two – a disturbing change in our frame of mind that's the direct consequence of too much technological success.

We have reached a point where wilderness is no longer a threat to us, where the wild itself has become something endangered. To some extent this wildness consists of the tangible things that constitute the natural world: the flora and fauna around us, the air we breathe, the water we drink, the earth we trod. Yet there is another facet to wildness, an intangible aspect that stirs deep within us. And that's precisely what rises to the surface whenever we allow it to do so, whenever we are in a place that cultivates it, when we are in a truly wild place. In such places, it is easy to question our civilizing tendencies and wonder what is happening to us as a consequence of them. What is gained in the process? What is being lost?

It does no good to disparage civilization as a whole, or the various cultures that have arisen from it during the past ten thousand years. Likewise we do ourselves a great disservice when we write off our distant ancestors as troglodytes incapable of appreciating art or sophisticated ideas. These polarities insult the wisdom of the ages, thus devaluating the human. There is more to being human than most of us are willing to believe. There is more to being human than accumulating great surpluses of food, making tools, devising complex systems of interaction or embracing some credo. Much more. And in wild places, in those places similar to where humanity emerged, there is room enough to see this. Exposure to the wild opens the mind.

Before continuing my hike along the Northville/Placid Trail, I spent a day at West Lake doing a lot of nothing, simply grooving with the natural world. I jotted down random thoughts in a notebook while lounging in the rocks along the shoreline. I daydreamed while enjoying the company of dragonflies. I stripped off all my clothes and went for a swim, getting clean in more ways than one. I tended a small campfire long after fixing dinner, just to watch its flames dance. That cleared my head. "What did you do out there?" people often ask when I tell them that I just spent several days in the woods. Bagging peaks, catching fish, and hiking trails end-to-end are activities that make sense to the average urbanite. After all, they are appropriately goal-oriented. But to just be there? What for? What's the sense in that? I usually don't succeed when I try to explain it. Truth is, some of the best things in life can't be explained. They have to be experienced.

I wish I could articulate the great wild silence, putting into words the way it consumes me. I long to vocalize the unfiltered reality of nature, thereby making it intelligible to empire builders, dreamers of heavenly cities, and other utterly urban folk. But that's not how it goes. Some people are in tune with their wild selves, others are not. And words cannot bridge the gap between them. Words can't even bridge the gap between one hiker and another. Two people can travel through the woods together and have entirely different walks: one experiencing a wild epiphany while the other merely swats mosquitoes and longs for the comforts of civilization. The great wild silence isn't for everyone. It speaks only to those who are ready and willing to listen.

There is a limit to how much one can talk about wildness without sounding foolish. Countless artists have tried to capture the wild on canvas only to caricaturize it. Countless poets have rendered it silly and dreamlike. Misty mountains, roaring waterfalls, soaring eagles and all the rest of it – the sublime becomes a cliché all too easily. And our stories aren't much better. The high drama of wilderness survival is entertaining enough, but that too misses the point. After all, it's the small, inconsequential aspects of the wild world that reach deep within us, rocking us to the very core of our being.

I like the company of children when I go into the woods. Adults carry too much baggage with them. Adults are all wrapped up in their desires, distracted by workaday lives, stifled by all the rules of social engagement both written and unwritten. Children, on the other hand, live in the moment. Dogs even more so. They may not interpret the silence the same way a brooding thinker like me does, but they rarely miss the hoot of an owl in the distance or a passing chipmunk. And therein lies the beauty of their wild encounters. Their wildness is straightforward, more earthbound. Their wildness runs much closer to the surface.

In 2008 I returned to the West Canada Lake Wilderness. This time I went only as far as Sampson Lake. Once again I sat for a day, and once again I sensed something about the world around me that's greater than myself. One of these days I'm going to go deep into the woods and stay there for a week or more, doing as little as I did when I was in the Alaskan bush. That will be a rewarding outing, no doubt. But I won't have much to write about afterward. The great wild silence renders an attentive listener mute every time. There is no expression that doesn't trivialize it. There are no words or manmade images that can adequately describe the phenomenon. It is, by definition, unspeakable.

Immersed in Wildness

A wild urge stirred deep within. That's why I loaded my pack and headed for Brooktrout Lake as soon as I could swing three days away from work. Brooktrout Lake is located in the heart of West Canada Lakes Wilderness in the south-central Adirondacks – a huge pocket of trackless forest that few people ever visit. The High Peaks Region to the north, with its big mountains and grand views, attracts tens of thousands of hikers every year. Spectacular country, no doubt. But for those of us craving wilderness solitude, there are better places to go.

The twenty-mile dirt road winding through the Moose River Recreation Area set the right mood. The sight and smell of the surrounding forest unraveled my nerves as the car rolled along at fifteen miles an hour. I spotted a deer feeding in a glade, and braked for a dozen turkeys crossing the road. Reaching the trailhead mid-afternoon, I parked the car, shouldered my pack then set forth. I whistled to my German Shepard dog Matika to follow. Didn't have to whistle twice.

The lush understory dampened my pants half an hour down the narrowing trail. Heavy rain had fallen around midday and the forest was still dripping wet. I was sweating profusely by then as well. The midsummer heat had turned the forest into a steam bath. Deer flies attacked my dog and me whenever we took a water break. No matter. I reveled in the endless green world enveloping me.

Red efts crawled across the muddy trail. The deep blue petals of closed gentian illuminated the forest floor, along with the starburst white of tall meadow rue. I signaled Matika to stay back as we approached a beaver pond, hoping to spot its inhabitant. No such luck. The pond remained silent and still beneath a formless white sky. The sharp click of my trekking poles against rocks resounded through the birches, spruces and firs towering overhead. The tributaries of Wolf Creek blathered incessantly as they rushed downhill. I was happy to listen.

The six-mile hike went fast. Soon I spotted Brooktrout Lake peeking through the trees. At the shelter on the far end of the lake, I ran into a pleasant twenty-something couple settling in for the evening. I chatted with them briefly then backtracked half a mile to a relatively flat place not far from the water's edge. There I pitched my tarp and made camp. A wood thrush sang it's flute-like song, welcoming me.

Down by the lake, I pumped water into my bottles while watching the sun slowly sink behind the nearby ridge. Dragonflies darted back and forth over blueberry bushes along the shoreline, catching mosquitoes. Matika rested on a fallen tree, taking in the scene. When the mosquitoes came out in force, we slipped underneath the netting hanging down from my tarp. The loud cry of a solitary loon echoed across the lake as darkness swallowed the forest.

At daybreak a raven croaked loudly overhead, startling Matika. Chipmunks chattered. Nuthatches and chickadees chirped away. After splashing water into my face, I watched a pair of loons swimming and diving just off shore. Matika would have gone after them had they been on land. I enjoyed a long, lazy breakfast then grabbed map, compass and water bottle before taking a short walk over to West Lake. Matika discovered all kinds of interesting smells along the way.

While standing on a big rock overlooking West Lake, I recalled previous excursions into this sprawling wilderness. On the far shore I had stopped to rest for a couple days during an end-to-end hike along the Northville/Placid Trail. Years before that, I had camped at Cedar Lakes a few miles farther east before venturing north to Lost Pond. A couple years ago I had sojourned at Sampson Lake to the southeast long enough for the wild to reclaim me. Now here I was completing circle.

A hermit named French Louie lived in these woods a century ago, hunting, trapping, and tending a subsistence garden. He built a cabin on West Lake and had lean-tos at Twin Lakes and elsewhere. I could never live alone like that for years on end, divorced from the rest of humankind, but I understand the attraction of deep forest solitude. It's a lot easier to be clear-headed and stress-free out here than it is in the developed lowlands.

The day was shaping up to be another warm one. Immediately upon returning to camp, I stripped off my clothes and waded into Brooktrout Lake. Matika watched from shore, belly down to cool mud. I hesitated while standing thigh-deep in the chilly water, eventually screwing up courage enough to take the plunge. Then the transformation was complete. I swam about frog-like for quite some time before emerging from the lake my old self – the same wild man who had banged around the Alaskan bush twenty years earlier. Along with a layer of dirt and sweat, I had just washed off something else.

Wildness is like that. Once it gets under your skin, it's hard to shake. A primal self quickly rises back to the surface whenever the setting is right. I suspect that the wild lies dormant within all of us, that even the most sophisticated urbanites aren't as far removed from nature as they think they are. After all, our bodies are made of the same elements found in the wildest, most remote places. The earth and our humanity are inexorably entwined. That's why places like the West Canada Lakes Wilderness are so important. In country like this it's easy to sense our link to the world.

That afternoon, I sat against a spruce tree, occasionally scribbling in my journal while watching the loons at play. A pair of canoeists came out of nowhere, crossed the lake then disappeared. Once my hyperactive mind settled down, I entered that nether region between daydreams and conscious thought. There I dwelled for the rest of the afternoon. Following a simple dinner of ramen noodles and trail mix, I continued the same thread while staring into a small campfire. Matika chased a chipmunk then satisfied her primal urges by chewing on a stick. The sun went down sooner than expected. Both man and dog went down shortly thereafter.

The next day I lingered over breakfast, reluctant to break camp. When finally I shouldered my pack and got back on the trail, I was glad to be on the move again – almost as glad as Matika was. The hike out went very fast. I stopped by the beaver pond again but its inhabitant still didn't show. No matter. Wandering through the woods on a beautiful summer day was all I needed or wanted.

Upon reaching the car, I wiped the sweat from my brow with an already sweat-soaked bandana then said goodbye to my favorite wilderness. I'd return soon, I promised myself, and the long drive back to pavement and buildings was pleasant enough. But I'm always a little sad whenever I leave the woods. For some of us, the wild isn't an abstraction.

Campfires and Bear Cans

The forest floor around the lean-to at Brooktrout Lake is trampled flat and picked clean of fallen branches, making the place look more like an overused campground than a deep woods retreat. I could range out a hundred yards or so for firewood but decide to camp elsewhere instead. After all, this isn't what I had in mind when I left my car at the trailhead and started the six-mile hike to get here.

Halfway around the lake, I drop my pack on a relatively flat stretch of ground and declare it home for the next couple days. It takes ten minutes to push back the deadwood so that I can set up a tarp and clear enough space for a fire circle. The lake is in sight but I am far enough away from the trail to confuse my canine companion, Matika. That's how I know that I've picked a good spot.

Several years earlier, while thru hiking the Northville-Placid Trail, I stayed in shelters. After hiking all day, all I wanted to do was flop somewhere – the more convenient, the better. But this time I want to make camp in the truest sense of the word. This time I am staying put after a relatively short hike. I am here to savor the wildness only sampled before.

With the woods still damp from a cloudburst at noon and the midsummer air still very warm, I decide against building a fire this evening. Besides, the mosquitoes are coming out. I eat a granola bar along with some trail mix, calling that dinner. Afterward I tie my food bag to the end of a rope slung over a tree branch overhead. That will keep my food out of reach of any bear that might come along. I've been doing this for thirty-odd years and it hasn't failed me yet. The trick, of course, is to get the bag suspended high into the air, away from any overhanging branches. I perfected the method when I was in the Alaskan bush so it's second nature to me now. But I must admit, slinging food bags this way isn't always easy to do.

Once everything in my camp is covered, I slip under the net dangling from my tarp. I listen to mosquitoes whine while darkness descends. The air is perfectly still. Matika snuggles into my side as I drift slowly into the land of dreams. Just past midnight, a loon's manic call breaks the deep silence, shocking me awake. Only then do I become fully aware of the wildness all around me.

There was a time when going to the Adirondacks meant a trip to the High Peaks Region to bag as many peaks as possible. I went there with friends, climbing Mt. Haystack, Algonquin, Mt. Marcy, and so on. I also explored Indian Pass, Lake Colden and Avalanche Pass with my brother. As a hiking guide, I lead small groups to Indian Lake and other popular spots. It's all magnificent country, no doubt. But when the Powers that Be put a ban on campfires in the region and required backpackers to carry bear cans, I stopped going there.

My last foray into the Eastern High Peaks was a three-day excursion into the Dix Wilderness. I carried a bear resistant canister during that trip. I found the hard plastic can cumbersome yet strangely convenient. No wonder it is required there now. The Eastern High Peaks is a magnet for novice hikers. Surely they find it a lot easier to carry bear cans than to sling food bags in trees, which most of them wouldn't do, anyhow. Still it doesn't feel right to me. Seems like a bear can is just another contraption, like a GPS or a camp stove, carried into the woods to compensate for lack of basic backcountry skills or understanding. Isn't there a better way to go?

The Eastern High Peaks are so overwhelmed by hikers that extreme measures must be taken to preserve what's left of the wilderness experience that one can have there. Bear cans reduce the number of incidents between bears and people, and the ban on campfires lessens the impact that backpackers have on high-use camping areas. Other rules, like the leash law, keep out-of-control dogs from harassing hikers. It all makes perfect sense. Still I'd rather go elsewhere in the Adirondacks where such measures aren't necessary.

A thru hike on the Northville-Placid Trail was a real eye-opener for me. The NPT traverses five major wilderness areas and wild forests, skirting dozens of pristine lakes and ponds, passing through climax forests and sprawling bogs as it arcs through the greater part of the Adirondacks. Most peak-baggers don't even know about it. As a consequence, traffic on the NPT is relatively light. I have hiked it all day and seen no more than half a dozen people. When one has that much backcountry to ones self, a bona fide wilderness experience is virtually guaranteed.

During my second day at Brooktrout Lake, I do a lot of nothing. I go for a short day hike, swim a little, take a nap. I spend most of the afternoon sitting against a tree, lost in thought as loons dive for fish. In the evening I build a fire the size of a pie pan, boiling up water for ramen noodles and tea. Matika pulls a stick from my woodpile and chews it to pieces. Afterward I stare into the campfire, letting my mind wander.

I go down with the sun. Having consumed too much tea, I am forced out of bed in the middle of the night. I look up and see a few stars peeking through the forest canopy. Then I catch a whiff of wild earth stirred up by a gentle breeze. I listen intently for the mechanical sound of civilization but hear nothing, nothing at all. The silence is both disarming and delightful.

In the morning of my third day out, I break down the fire circle, bury the ashes and slowly make my camp disappear. A loaded pack leans against an old birch when I'm done. Dead branches and other forest duff scattered about the site conceal the fact that I have spent time here. I shoulder the pack then go, whistling for Matika to follow. She leaps forward all smiles, ready for whatever the day brings.

The naturalist John Burroughs went camping in the Adirondacks when he was a young man. In an essay about it he wrote: "Better than fish or game or grand scenery, or any adventure by night or day, is the wordless intercourse with rude Nature one has on these expeditions." I couldn't agree more. As I tramp through the forest, relishing all of its sights, sounds, and smells, I feel a connection with something greater than myself. As I grow older, I feel less inclined to name that something, or to say anything about what we ought or ought not to do regarding it. Like my dog, I am happy enough just being in the moment, running wild for a little while.

Deep Forest Ruminations

1

Dark clouds loom over the horizon directly ahead. Earlier this morning the sky turned blue after a short drive through heavy rain just south of my home in northern Vermont. That led me to believe I was slipping south of the storm track. But now it's obvious that my six-day retreat into the Adirondack backcountry is going to start out wet. Oh well. I've waited too long for this outing to cancel or even delay it. Despite the dire warnings of weather forecasters, I'm going into the woods.

Drizzle turns into heavy rain as the town of Indian Lake appears. I pull into a convenience store parking lot then go inside to get a junk food lunch. I take it back to the car where Matika, my long-haired German Shepherd, eagerly awaits. She's all smiles, knowing that my loaded backpack is right behind her. She doesn't care where we are going or what the weather is. I place a bowl of kibble on the back seat. When she's done I fill the bowl with water. She splashes it everywhere as she drinks. I eat a hot dog as the storm intensifies. When the downpour diminishes to light rainfall, I tap out a message on my cell phone, informing my wife Judy that I'm going for it. I told her that I'd check into a motel if the weather became too severe, but "severe" is a relative word.

Back on the road, I drive south fifteen more miles before leaving pavement. A wide, graded dirt road eases around Mason Lake then snakes three miles to a place on my map called Perkins Clearing. There I turn onto a narrow, unimproved, dirt road that winds through the forest another three miles to the trailhead. I have a saw in the back of my car just in case I have to cut away a downed tree in order to reach my destination. Hope that's not necessary. When the dirt road drops to a low spot, I get out and wade across the large pool of water in the way, making sure my little hatchback can splash through it. Then I continue the ten-mile-an-hour drive up a partially washed-out track. Eventually the trailhead parking lot appears.

After parking my car, I grab the saw. There's an SUV in the parking lot trapped behind a fallen tree. I cut away the upper branches so that its driver can get around the tree when he or she leaves the woods. The SUV is designed for tracks just like the one leading to this trailhead, but how many people carry a saw in their car?

Matika is ready to go. She doesn't carry a dog pack any more because her hips can't take it. So I hoist a fifty-pound pack to my shoulders – food and gear enough for both of us. Then I sign into the trailhead register, grab my hiking poles, and set forth into the West Canada Lakes Wilderness.

While finishing a grueling hike in northern Maine a few years back, I passed a beautiful wilderness pond glimmering on a partly cloudy, late summer day. Many times since then I've daydreamed about spending a week there. Seems like I'm always moving through the backcountry, never staying anywhere long enough in any one place to fully savor it. Passing through the woods is not the same as being in the woods. So I promised myself that someday I would hike in somewhere and stay put for a change. Then I'd be able to groove on the wild without distraction.

I did that Maine hike in 2009. Eight years have gone by since then. What have I been doing? Changing jobs, starting an online business, writing and publishing books, fixing up and selling my old house, moving, and a host of other distractions. Life is what happens while we're busy making other plans, and the years slip away. Now in my 60s, I'm finally getting around to making good on that promise to myself. And Matika is still by my side.

Matika was in her prime when she and I did that Maine hike. Now she's an old dog with the kind of hip problems that old dogs commonly get. Because of that we won't be going far. Four miles to Pillsbury Lake today, and another two miles to Whitney Lake tomorrow perhaps. She can handle that much. Not more. One could say that Matika's company guarantees that I'll be staying put somewhere. Truth is, I'd probably keep hiking hard, day after day, if I didn't have her by my side. After all, that's what I'm accustomed to doing.

I'm the kind of guy who has to be active, if not physically then mentally. Anticipating that, I've brought along a brand new field journal to fill with my thoughts while staying put. I'm a ruminator at heart.

Pondering imponderable paradoxes comes naturally to me. I'm particularly interested in the relationship between God, humankind and nature. I think about that all the time. To facilitate my ruminations, I've brought along some mental kindling. I copied 50 quotes from philosophers, theologians and naturalists into the back of my journal before leaving home. Any one of those quotes can set my mind on fire.

The rain isn't so bad. It's not heavy enough to warrant wearing raingear, anyhow. That's encouraging. All the same, I slip into a funk while hiking up the trail. While writing my name in the trail register a few minutes ago, I noticed that a couple hikers signed in yesterday, putting down Pillsbury Lake as their destination. And they're out for three days. I was hoping to have that place all to myself. With heavy rain saturating the ground at midday, setting up my tarp this evening is pretty much out of the question. That means I'll have to stay in the Pillsbury Lake Shelter tonight. That's probably where they're going to be. I stab the muddy trail with my walking poles as I press forward, venting my frustration. Then I consider my options. I'll have stay in the shelter tonight, but tomorrow I could camp somewhere on the other side of the lake, or continue to Whitney Lake. There's no marked trail to Whitney Lake so I should be alone there. I don't go into the woods to socialize but one evening of it will be okay. Tonight only. Most backcountry travelers make good campfire companions. It'll be okay.

Twenty minutes into the hike, I cut my pace. I'm in for the long haul. Matika creeps out in front of me. The rain has diminished to a drizzle. Or maybe what's coming down is just water dripping from the trees. Hard to say. Either way it's 100% humidity in these woods right now, and I've already worked up a good sweat. Yeah, I'm getting wet, but the air is relatively cool and the bugs are down so I can't complain. Feels good to be on a trail again, going deep into a wilderness area.

After hiking two miles, I reach a trail junction. A big sign points left, to the west. It says: French Louie Trail. That's new. The sign wasn't here the last time I came this way. But that was several years ago. A short break at the junction then Matika and I head west. French Louie Trail narrows considerably as it climbs. Then it flattens to an endless series of mud holes. The clouds overhead break open, exposing a patch of blue sky, but there's still thunder rumbling in the distance. And water is still dripping through the trees. On a downward slope, the trail is practically a stream. No trail maintenance crew has come this way lately. Matika has some trouble negotiating the downed trees blocking the way. I lead her around the downed trees when I can, and lift her over them when I can't. At 80 pounds, lifting her is no mean feat for me, especially with a full pack still on my back.

As the trail skirts a wetland, it becomes overgrown and hard to follow. Matika slips behind me after losing her way in the high grass. The dripping vegetation soaks us both to the skin. Then comes the final leg to Pillsbury Lake with a brief glimpse of it glistening through the trees. I'm soft, heavy, and feeling decades of trail pounding in my joints, but I've almost reached my destination for the day. A sign pointing towards the shelter appears soon enough. I take the trail leading to it.

While approaching the shelter, I brace myself for an encounter with its occupants. Matika stays behind me. I spot the back end of the shelter through the dense understory ahead. There's no doubt in my mind now that this is where my dog and I should spend the night. Distant thunder is drawing closer. I ease around the corner of the shelter to its opening, ready to project a smile and utter a friendly greeting. To my great surprise, it's empty. I drop my pack in the shelter then look around for tents. Nothing. There's no one here.

A nearby path leads to the lake's edge. I scramble down it, expecting to see tents on the opposite shore. Still nothing. On the way back to the shelter, though, I spot a swarm of bees coming out of the ground. Sure enough, I'm stung once on the way up the path and again in front of the shelter. Damn! So much for that lake access. I'll have to find another place to draw water.

Looking around the shelter for a journal or some other clue as to what happened to the couple that's supposed to be here, I find nothing but four large stones strewn across the floor. They obviously belong in the fire pit so that's where I put them. Then I sweep out the shelter with a towel I've brought with me to wipe down my dog. There's no broom here either. No sooner do I finish cleaning out the shelter then the rain starts coming down hard again. Matika makes herself comfortable at one end of the shelter while I blow open my pack at the other. We have arrived.

2

The rain beats against the shelter roof as I string up my mosquito bar – a rectangular net big enough to cover a camper's cot. I usually set it up beneath my tarp, but it works in shelters just as well. The mosquitoes aren't bad yet but I'm sure they will be. This has been a wet summer so far. Ideal conditions for those little buggers to breed. I'm sure the other blood-sucking creatures will also come out once the rain stops. Ah, nature!

I string a line from one shelter wall to the next to air dry the dog towel after using it on Matika. Then I hang up my other wet things. I switch from a damp t-shirt to a dry one. Won't get out of these wet pants and boots until later, after fetching water. I hang up the backpack cover. It did a great job keeping my gear from getting soaked. Out of a worn, old backpack I pull a sleeping bag, foam pad, camp stove, and a few other essentials. A little sorting and organizing then suddenly this shelter is home sweet home. I've taken over the left half of it, leaving the other half clear just in case someone else comes along.

The sun is peeking through the clouds. Water drips from the roof edge, pooling immediately in front of the shelter. It drips from the surrounding conifers as well. A patch of blue sky appears as the rain tapers off. Soon I hear a white-throated sparrow, a veery, a nuthatch, and other songbirds. The moss and lichen clinging to the conifers gives this place a rainforest look. Mist partially obscures Noisey Ridge – the wooded hill on the opposite side of the lake.

I pull my cell phone out of a plastic bag then check it. No service. Now it's just a fancy timepiece.

Six o'clock already. Time to get dinner going. I turn off my phone to conserve battery power then put it back in the bag.

Before fixing dinner I clean out the fire pit. It's full of trash, charred chunks of wood, and half-burnt logs three to four feet long – a real eyesore. I collect the trash, stack the big logs neatly off to the side, and create a pile of birch bark and smaller chunks of wood to burn up later. No campfire this evening, though. The dead wood scattered across the forest floor is way too wet for that. In a pinch I could get a fire going, but there's no need for it right now. I'll build one tomorrow.

Dinner is an expedient affair. I fire up the camp stove then open my food bags. The stove hisses loudly in the forest silence. Soon I have enough hot water for tea and a dehydrated meal. While waiting for the meal to reconstitute, I feed Matika two cups of kibble that I've poured into one of the two pans of my mess kit. She gets one pan; I get the other. If I'm paying attention, I won't confuse the two. But that's been known to happen.

After dinner I walk down to the lake's edge, looking for a good place to collect water. Oddly enough, Matika stays in the shelter. She must be really tired. The closest lake access is out of the question since that's where the bees live. I find two other places a little farther away. One of them is suitable for pumping water so I set to work, filling two bottles. I take in the view while doing so. The placid lake surface is dimpled by hatching flies, then by a thin drizzle. Conifers rise from the far shore. Grey clouds swirl low overhead. I cap the bottles before heading back to the shelter.

Matika stretches across the shelter floor while I lean against the wall using a rolled up sleeping bag for back support. Out comes my journal, along with bug dope that I slather on Matika and myself. I don't resort to bug dope unless it's absolutely necessary, but this is definitely a year to do so. The mosquitoes are coming out in force now, along with black flies and no-see-ums.

Rain gently falls through late evening sunlight. Water drips from everything. It's a soothing sound, actually, now that I'm comfortably ensconced in a shelter that's nice and dry. I break open my field journal and start writing in it while sipping tea and munching gourmet jellybeans. Matika closes her eyes.

At long last, I've done it. I've come to a place deep in the wilderness to hang out for six days and do a lot of nothing. No big hiking adventure, no agenda, no plans. Maybe I'll move over to Whitney Lake in a day or two; maybe I'll stay right here. It doesn't matter. The main thing is to follow my moods as closely as possible. I have six days just to groove on the wild, observe, relax, think, and write.

Amazing how quiet it is here. Deep woods silence always comes as something of a shock the first day. The dripping forest, an occasional songbird, a chipmunk chattering, a pine siskin stealing in and out of camp, and the sound of something that I can't quite identify. Is that a stream in the distance or the collective hum of so many insects buzzing around? I can just barely hear it. The wild closes in around me – a subtle yet irresistible force.

I've come out here to contemplate the relationships between God, humankind and nature, and see how well my outdoor thoughts sync with my indoor ones. Yeah, that was my intention. But right now that seems like a bad idea. Right now it feels like I should simply be here, completely immersed in the moment. Why? Because nature insists upon it. Because nature is more than my abstractions. Because nature has no opinions, no philosophy or religion. It just is.

Dusk. Matika raises her head all of a sudden, ears up and nose twitching. What does she hear? What does she smell? A wood thrush sings from a nearby tree branch, welcoming me back to the wild. Then there's a loud, watery *thunk!* as if someone just threw a large stone into the lake. I spot a beaver swimming close to shore. He's not happy about Matika and me being here. He flaps his tail while diving, creating another loud *thunk!* to warn others about our intrusion. Frogs croak from the reedy shoreline – bullfrogs, green frogs and others. The last light of day fades away.

I brush my teeth right before going to bed. Beneath the mosquito net, Matika snuggles into my side. I finish writing in my journal by headlamp, trying to record everything that has happened today. Croaking frogs and dripping woods lull me to sleep.

In the middle of the night I hear the long, incredibly loud, lonely call of a loon somewhere on the lake. Lonely? That's how it strikes me, anyhow. I'm completely alone out here, just me and my dog that is, and the all-encompassing wildness is anything but comforting. That's because I'm still new to this place, still fresh from the developed lowlands full of people, still feeling way too civilized to relate to the wild just yet. Give it time.

3

Daybreak. Mist clings to the opposite shore. The top of Noisey Ridge has disappeared into a formless grey sky. The lake is perfectly still. Matika and I both go out to pee then return to bed, taking our sweet time waking up. Soon mosquitoes are whining just outside the netting, waiting for us to come out and play. Matika snuggles into my side, until stretching out across the shelter floor seems like a better idea. Then she escapes the net, offering herself to the mosquitoes.

The loon I heard last night calls out loud and clear, right before leaving the lake. A sparrow sings a simple five-note song over and over, as if it has nothing better to do. Other songbirds chirp and sing from the surrounding trees. Frogs make clicking sounds as they croak down by the water's edge. The vegetation is thick around camp, except for a small grassy spot off to the left. The forest is fecund. Even the ground is teeming with life forms. I recently read somewhere that every tablespoon of rich forest soil contains over a billion microbes. Yeah, the word "fecund" doesn't even begin to cover what's going on out here.

Eventually I leave the net, get dressed then lower the food bags dangling from a line that I slung into the trees last night. Matika is excited about eating. I fire up my stove and start boiling water for tea before feeding her. After she eats, she drinks nearly a liter of water, slopping a good part of it out of the pan. Hmm… I'll have to pump more after breakfast. Matika makes more work for me, but I don't mind too much. I prefer her company to that of people whenever I'm in the woods. There's much to be gained by an interspecies relationship. It puts things in perspective. Unlike me, Matika is firmly ensconced in the here/now. And she always keeps things simple.

Mosquitoes buzz around me as I eat breakfast then putter about camp. I wave most of them away, killing only the ones that land on my exposed skin. Every once in a while, one takes her measure of blood. Mosquitoes remind me that I cannot live forever. Eventually one of them will transfer some deadly disease to me with not-so-benign indifference. I can only protect myself up to a point. If the mosquitoes don't get me, then a virus, bacteria, or something else will. That's God's will – nature's way. What am I but a blip in time, a temporary knot of being in this world? A creature like me lives ninety years or less. Most likely less. Like every other living thing out here, my days are numbered. I'd better make good use of them.

The mist dissipates. Rainwater, still clinging to leaves, glistens in the early morning sunlight. Birches, red spruce and balsam firs surround the shelter. Some of the conifers are dead or dying. I'm not sure why. Songbirds draw closer, flitting from tree to tree. They are easy to spot on the denuded branches. A chipmunk peeks from the thick vegetation along the camp's edge. A small squirrel sitting on a branch loudly chews a spruce cone. Matika doesn't see it yet, but she will.

I pull out my map to see what the terrain looks like between here and Whitney Lake. It's only two miles away. Unlike this place, Whitney Lake is off the beaten path. That would be a better place to stay put, to sit and think. There I'm not likely so see anyone at all. I could move over to Whitney Lake today but no, my old dog needs a rest. Maybe tomorrow. Yeah, stay here today. Slow down. Try to get in sync with the wild. There's no reason to rush. I'm not in the bustling lowlands any more.

This shelter has been here a while. Its roof is covered with moss. The roof's drip edge is rotted and uneven. Hundreds of names and dates have been carved into the shelter walls. Many date back to the 90s and 80s. A few go back to the 70s and 60s. One fellow has scratched a succession of dates reaching back as far as the 50s, starting with the year I was born. Someone else wrote "Hiram 1923." That can't be real. I don't quite understand this need to leave a mark on a shelter wall. To let the world know that one has been here perhaps? As for me, well, I've never carved my name in a shelter and never will. I like to pass through the forest like a ghost.

Tea finished, water pumped, and camp all nice and tidy. I'm just about ready to explore the area immediately around the shelter, but first things first: write down a few thoughts. I prop my foam pad and rolled sleeping bag against the shelter wall to make a comfortable place to sit. Then I crack open my journal, reading some of the quotes copied there.

The Trappist monk Thomas Merton once wrote: "The things that we love tell us what we are." I love the wild forest, the pursuit of truth, and putting my thoughts down on paper. Or, as I like to say whenever someone asks me to describe myself: I wander, I wonder, I write.

First and foremost, I love the wild. Some people feel uneasy deep in the woods, but I am more at home here than anywhere else. It's hard to say why exactly. I have no illusions about wildness. I do not see Mother Nature as some benign force always drawing things into balance and harmony. It has its darker side to be sure: tooth, claw and all that. Not to mention the many challenges it presents: storms, heat, hypothermia, etc. I spend a good part of my time out here attending to physical needs. Then there's the food I bring with me that has to be kept away from other critters before it reaches my belly. That too can be a challenge. All the same, I love wandering freely through a wild and beautiful forest. Can't imagine a better place to be.

Love of truth? That's why I call myself a philosopher. I long to know what the world really is aside from all preconceptions about it, even if what I discover is deeply unsettling. How is the love of truth any different from the love of wildness? How can there be truth without some basic understanding of nature? I'm convinced that any philosopher who doesn't wonder about the nature of nature isn't getting to the heart of the matter. In wildness lies the truth of the world. Everything else stems from that.

As for writing, well, for me that's also an act of discovery. After extensive wandering and wondering, I simply put down on paper what I find immediately around me, what I discover about the world at large, and whatever I learn about myself in the process. So there it is: I love the truth, the wild, and writing about it. That's who/what I am. So in my case, anyhow, Merton was right.

A small songbird with a bright yellow belly comes to visit while I'm writing in my journal. It's a warbler of some sort, I think. A toad appears. The loon pops into view, floating carefree in the middle of the lake. The natural world goes about its business as I sit here pondering things.

Mid-morning. Time to scout the area. Matika is all for it. I turn left when leaving the shelter, passing my water access and a couple worn campsites full of exposed roots. The sketchy trail underfoot splits into several narrow forage paths that have been picked clean of firewood. They all fade into the understory. There's no really good place here to camp so I head the other direction, going east of the shelter. That's where the outhouse is located. Looks like it could use some attention. No place to camp over here, either. From the water's edge, I glass the opposite shore with my binoculars. Don't see a good place to camp over there. No easy access to the water in sight, anyhow. Hmm… Guess I'll stay right where I am.

Time to collect firewood. I hike out to the main trail then turn west, collecting a few sticks the thickness of my thumb along the way. Everything is still wet from yesterday's rain so I strip the bark off the sticks that I gather. That'll make them dry faster. I don't travel far before reaching a flooded low spot in the trail next to a beaver pond. That prompts me to head the other direction. I hike east a hundred yards, past the side trail to the shelter, and find a couple large downed trees. Perfect! I break off an armload of sticks, thumb-sized or thicker. Then I carry it all back to the shelter. Now I have enough wood for several fires. I dump the sticks next to the fire pit and let the sun finish drying them.

I'm wet again, having brushed against soaked vegetation while collecting wood. And the stuff I hung out to dry last night is still damp. No matter. A gentle breeze is now wafting across the lake and through the trees. That'll dry things out eventually. It'll keep the bugs at bay as well. The overhead clouds are moving away quickly. The sky is mostly blue now. It's turning into a beautiful, midsummer day.

A pileated woodpecker calls out. It's not far away. Butterflies flutter through camp. Matika, ears up and attentive, watches a squirrel scrambling across a tree branch. The rippled surface of the lake reflects sunlight. The air is noticeably warmer now, with temps in the high 70s.

Pillsbury Lake is a sweet place. Do I really need to move over to Whitney Lake? Can't imagine it being any better than this. Then again, I can't imagine staying here for the next five days. Staying put seemed like a good idea when I was pounding the trail through Maine eight years ago, but now I wonder if I can handle it. What will I *do* with all my time? Staying put is a lot harder than it sounds. Maybe I'll hike around a little just to keep things interesting. Tomorrow I'll go over to Whitney Lake and check it out. That'll help me decide whether or not to move there. If nothing else, the day hike will feel good.

4

After a simple lunch and a short nap, I decide to do exactly what I came here to do: stay put. It's the one thing I've never done. Actually, I did just that 25 years ago, when I was in the Alaskan bush. I had planned on bushwhacking deep into the wilderness during that two-week sojourn, but ended up staying close to my base camp instead. Since then I've been on the move, never staying more than two days in one place during any given outing. Well, it's time to change that. Barring encroachment by any other backpackers that might come along, I'll stay right here. A day hike to Whitney Lake would be nice, but I don't have to move over there. Pillsbury Lake is just fine. It's just as good a place as any to sit and think and groove on nature.

A four-mile hike then staying put. I wonder if I could have managed this had it not been for my old dog. Matika, with her bad hips, makes it easier for me to dial it back. On my own I'd probably hike 20 miles or more during this outing. That's what I'm in the habit of doing, anyhow. But no, not this time. This time it's all about the fusion of the abstract and the concrete, making my worldview sync with wild reality inasmuch as that is possible. Where to begin? I already have. I began the moment I cracked open my field journal and started jotting down these thoughts.

Philosophy – the love of wisdom, the pursuit of truth. I claim to love truth but the truth is I'm just as afraid of it as the next guy. The first and foremost truth: I'm going to die someday. Being fully cognizant of that event, *before* the fact, is what sets me apart from the other animals. It's the combined curse of self-awareness and foresight – the very attributes that have enabled my kind to prosper over the millennia. All other creatures may suspect as much, but they obviously go about their business without giving the matter much thought. But we, *Homo sapiens*, dwell upon it.

Mortality is a terrible truth. Regardless what any of us might believe about the afterlife, death is final. It is not a revolving door through which one passes, back and forth. Oh sure, sometimes we entertain notions of the dead coming back to haunt those of us still living, but that's all in our heads. And stories concerning those who have resurrected always have a supernatural aspect to them. In nature, in the world that you and I live, death is final. It is built into the very definition of living. All living things die eventually. And when we pass through that door, we don't come back.

With this awareness comes the urge to find or create meaning in life – another distinctly human attribute. A few of the simpler approaches: be good during this life and go to heaven afterward; or just live in the moment; or work hard and accrue as much wealth as you can. Other more sophisticated approaches vary greatly, from elaborate rational constructs of meaning to nihilistic dismissals of meaning altogether. But all of these worldviews – philosophies and religions both simple and complex – address the fundamental truth of the human condition: we are all going to die. With that in mind, some of us can't help but ask: What is it all for? Why do we exist in the first place? Why does anything exist?

If life implies death, then death implies meaning. Not just the meaning of my life or anyone else's, but the meaning of all living things, of life in general. What is the meaning and purpose of nature as a whole and why did it come to be? No matter how *sapient* we may think we are, this is the one question that none of us can definitively answer. Oh sure, we have our elaborate theories, beliefs and rationalizations, but none of us knows the answer with absolute certainty. To know that we would have to know what nature truly is. And that level of understanding, as our scientists make crystal clear, is not ours – at least not yet.

We know a great deal about the many working parts of nature, but nature as a whole remains beyond our comprehension. "Nature contains that which does not concern us, and has no intention of taking us into its confidence," the renowned essayist Loren Eiseley wrote after pondering this matter at length. In other words, nature is greater than we are. It existed long before we arrived on the scene, and will exist long after we are gone no matter how much we stir things up. Not just nature as the web of life on this planet, but nature as a whole – universal nature, the nature of the cosmos at large, Nature with a capital "N." We have only begun to plumb its depths, to unravel its mysteries.

Matika chews a stick while I entertain my abstractions. She gets a piece of wood stuck between her teeth and can't get it out. I go over and put my nimble fingers to the task but to no avail. Looking around in her mouth, I don't see the offending wood chip.

The passage of time... All living things are finite. My canine companion will not live more than another year or two. My aging parents, now in their late 80s, have myriad health problems so they probably won't live much longer. My wife Judy and I, according to the law of averages, will probably live another 20 years or so. Then again, who knows what tomorrow will bring? Life is chock full of surprises. That's especially true when it comes to death. Any one of us could die at any given moment. So what can we do but live our lives fully here and now? The past is certain because it's finished. The future is anyone's guess.

Science is the construction of knowledge with the building blocks of the past. What *has* occurred is known, or what can be known to some extent. What *will* occur can be extrapolated from this, surely, but not with absolute certainty. Every weather forecast, for example, has an element of uncertainty. That's why I laugh whenever someone says that there's 100% chance of rain tomorrow. 99.9% perhaps, but not 100%. The best guess is still a guess. Science is only an educated guess. As for philosophy and religion, well, that's guesswork for sure.

Once again Matika paws at her mouth, trying to loosen that piece of wood stuck in her teeth. I stop writing in my journal long enough to go over and help her. This time I spot the wood chip wedged in a large gap between a premolar and a molar. With a little patience I finally get my fingers on it, assuring Matika all the while that I have the situation under control. Trust. I trust that she won't bite me. She trusts that I won't hurt her. The wood chip comes out. Matika smiles.

I am shocked to find myself suddenly 61 years of age, sitting by a lake recalling 40-odd years of thinking, woods wandering, and scribbling down words like this. Has it really been five years since I last set foot in the West Canada Lakes Wilderness? Has Matika really been my hiking companion for over a decade? Is the backpack I'm using on this trip really 25 years old? Is the mess kit I'm using, acquired when I was a Boy Scout, really half a century old? Is the shelter I'm leaning against really older than me? How about the oldest trees standing around me? How long has this lake been here? How old are the rocks in the fire pit? When I think about the first plants and animals, I'm looking back in time half a billion years. Bacteria have been around a billion years or more. The planet I'm living on goes back 4.5 billion years. The universe as a whole is 14.7 billion years old, dating back to that singularity in spacetime from which everything emerged. Before that? Good lord, does it even matter?

It's buggy here. Flies, deer flies, black flies, bees, sweat bees, mosquitoes, gnats, etc. Matika is tormented more by them than I am. After all, I am distracted by my abstractions. So I put Matika under the mosquito net and make her lie down. Eventually she figures out that the bugs can't get to her there. Then she takes a nap. I return to my journal.

The passage of time… All things are finite. All things take place in time. Yet what happened more than a day ago is sometimes difficult to grasp. Tell me that I have always been camped here at this lake and a part of me will believe you – the part of me that lives in the eternal present. But the part of me that is aware of the passage of time will refute it, of course, recalling events that took place before I came here. My knowledge of natural history, geology and astronomy takes the passage of time to another level, beyond what I can experience directly. I am sapient about that much, anyhow.

The loon suddenly cries out, late in the afternoon, reminding me where I am. A steady, dreamy, midsummer breeze rolls out of the west. Bugs notwithstanding, it feels good to be here. I've visited better places than Pillsbury Lake – more beautiful lakes with deeper waters, better views and easier access – but this place is wild and that's all that matters. Wildness is all I need right now, not ease of access or better views. And a day like today is one to be remembered no matter what. A long summer day spent in the wild is a precious thing, indeed, no matter how achy, wet, dirty or bug-bitten one is.

Mayflies are hatching now. Some have slipped right into camp, along with a dragonfly, two ornery chipmunks, and a few toads. What a menagerie! Wood sorrel blooms along the camp's edge, along with some yellow and white flowers whose names I can't recall. I spot the telltale fruit of a blue bead lily not far away. Is it that time of year already? Wildflowers are a parade marching through the seasons. If I look away for just a moment or two, I'll miss something.

5

The food bags, dangling from a cord strung between the shelter and a nearby tree, aren't quite as full as they were this time yesterday. Like sand moving through an hourglass, they mark the passage of time. When the food is nearly gone, it'll be time to leave. I drop the bags then open them, commencing dinner. Matika is excited by the prospect, of course.

The sticks piled in front of the shelter are bone dry now, having baked in the sun all day. I start breaking them into foot-long pieces and stacking them neatly on the ground. Then I build a small tipi out of kindling and birch bark in the middle of the fire pit. Even though I have plenty of fuel on hand for the camp stove, I start a fire just big enough to boil a pot of water. It's important to keep up this skill. I might need it someday.

While still snapping sticks, I hear a rumbling in the distance. It sounds like approaching thunder. As it grows louder, it becomes apparent to me that whatever's making that sound isn't the least bit natural. I stop what I'm doing, alarmed by the intensity and increasing volume of it. A few seconds later, an attack helicopter sweeps around Noisey Ridge, just above the trees. Then it roars over the lake in full view, looking every bit like the death-dealing machine that it is: dark, metallic and menacing. A second one pops into view, right on the heels of the first. An unholy drone reverberates through the hills.

So much for wilderness solitude. Then again, those huge mechanical birds disappear just as quickly as they came, leaving me a bit shaken yet still tending my campfire. The sudden appearance of such fierce instruments of destruction remind me that life back in the developed lowlands is anything but ideal. I could make a good argument why such instruments are absolutely necessary, but that doesn't change the tragedy of it all. Collectively speaking, humankind is a wounded beast, and the wounds are self-inflicted. Desperate, dangerous and irrational, it doesn't know what is real or how to manage its own conflicting desires. That's why it's so important for individuals to come out here and get back in touch with the earth. What can one person do to stop the tragedy unfolding daily and help humankind heal once and for all? First and foremost, one must address one's own shortcomings, one's own flawed worldview. What can I do to heal myself once and for all? Probably not much, but it seems like I should at least try.

The campfire burns down a pile of glowing embers as I clean up the mess kit pans and sling the food bags back into the air. Matika has two cups of kibble in her belly; I have ramen noodles in mine. The sun is still high in the sky, so I'll wait a while before building another fire. The next one will be for pleasure only.

All my gear has been shoved into the left half of the shelter once again. This being Tuesday, a weekday, there probably aren't many hikers in the woods right now. All the same, I've cleared a space for anyone who might come along.

Two loons are making a scene at the far end of the lake. It's a mating pair, no doubt. Their enchanting calls echo through the forest. Through my binoculars I watch them a while as they dance together across the surface of the lake. I wonder if they'll be spending the night here.

The bugs that went away when I started the fire are back now. Matika goes under the net to escape them. What a quick study she is! I ignore them, waving away the worst offenders while making myself comfortable against the shelter wall. Then I crack open my field journal.

"What is communing with nature but communing with ourselves?" the naturalist John Burroughs once asked, "Nature gives back our thoughts and feelings, as we see our faces reflected in a pool." True, nature gives back our thoughts and feelings, but it's more than a mere reflection. We see ourselves in nature because we *are* nature – a part of it, anyhow. We see ourselves in nature because we don't really stand outside of it.

Nature and human nature are inextricably entwined. There's no definitive break between the two. Whatever we say about nature, we say about ourselves. Whatever we say about ourselves, we say about nature. To commune with nature is simply to go back to the source and remember who/what we are.

Yet there is something about *Homo sapiens* that is qualitatively different from the rest of nature. It all came about slowly, naturally, over great periods of time, but eventually we became something the world had never seen before. Our human-ness took a great leap forward 100,000 years ago when we first started burying our dead, and again roughly 40,000 years ago when we started painting on rock walls. Both of these activities indicate abstract thought. Language had something to do with it, no doubt. Culture arose. We began to share ideas, plan and organize. Soon we were cultivating plants and staying in one place instead of moving around all the time as hunter/gatherer societies usually do. We became town dwellers, *civil-ized*. Then our relationship with the wild changed dramatically. All of a sudden it was us versus them, man subduing nature, and eventually man subduing man. Our numbers increased exponentially, as did our problems. Civilization, what a concept!

We are civilized, yes, but not devoid of wildness. We are the masters of our own destiny, perhaps, but not completely cut off from nature – at least not yet. To some extent we remain just as wild as we once were despite all the structures, systems and rules that we have created for ourselves through the millennia.

Whenever I get half a chance, I cultivate my wildness. In forests that are left pretty much alone – designated wilderness areas and the like – I find this incredibly easy to do. I bring food, clothes and a few basic tools with me, but the wild seeps into me all the same. Wildness also emerges from deep within. And that's a good thing, I think. There are those who believe that our humanity is a victory over nature, a transcendence of it, but I do not share this view. On the contrary, I see our human-ness as something completely natural. And if ever we succeed in severing our ties the wild world once and for all, I believe we will lose an essential part of ourselves. As Burroughs said, in our communing with nature, we commune with ourselves. Completely divorced from it, we are lost.

Back to the source, if only for a few days... I keep my tools to a minimum. I walk, sweat, make fire, cook and eat my food, defecate, pee, sleep, get cleaned up (to minimize the filth), get angry, laugh, cry, become ecstatic, bleed, curse the bugs, slip and fall in the mud, celebrate the beauty and wonder of the world, try to stay warm, try to stay cool, drink lots of water, avoid water-borne diseases (however I can), live in the moment, live dangerously, experience fear then overcome it, run into obstacles and learn true humility, work things out, think ahead, accomplish tasks, fail, try again, acknowledge the great mystery, and sing. Then I share it all with others however I can.

The sun is just now setting. Already my dog is snoring. The world beyond her snores is quiet and still.

I'm no Luddite. Every day, back in the developed lowlands, I use electronic devices to work, play, and get on with my life. There are great advantages to using these tools, obviously. But they are only tools, no better or worse than knives, compasses or water filters. *Homo faber* – the hominid that makes things. Toolmakers we are, absolutely, but that's not all we are. There is more to creativity and innovation than making a lively campfire or building a better machine. We possess wild minds that enable us to see the world in remarkable ways. More to the point, we get fresh new ideas – ways of interacting with the world that aren't real until we make them real, like flying, deep diving, or going into space. We can *envision* something then make it happen. That gives us a special relationship with nature – to use her, abuse her, care for her, or destroy her as no other creature can. Our relationship with nature runs deeper than food and sex – those fundamental concerns of all animals. We are visionary, therefore more responsible for our actions than the rest of creation.

"All nature is my bride," Henry David Thoreau wrote in his journals. And that is the kind of relationship we should all have with the natural world. Collectively speaking, we should marry her. Technology as a false god. When we have an inordinate faith in tools, thinking that tools alone are the solution to all our problems, we falter. That's because it's our relationship with nature that really matters. It's our relationship with nature that will determine whether or not we truly prosper. In the greater scheme of things, it is our understanding of nature and our relationship with it that will determine our success or failure as a species.

I make a second campfire after sundown, just for the sheer pleasure of it. It's an elemental connection to the natural world – a form of worship you could say. Fire, water, earth, and sky. It is all here this evening – overhead, at my feet, and right before me. I burn up several thick chunks of charred wood left behind by others, along with a good portion of my snapped sticks. The afterglow in the western sky slowly fades in the process, narrowing my focus to the flames leaping before my eyes. A cloudless sky, the air absolutely still, and a fire burning smoke free. Once I've had enough of it, I use a stick to push half-burnt pieces of wood into the center of the fire. Then I add a few thinner, smaller sticks to burn it all down to embers, blowing on the diminishing flames all the while. With camp lit by an orange glow, I go about my bedtime routine, finally brushing my teeth and spitting toothpaste into the embers before dousing them with a pot of water. Then I crawl beneath the net, joining Matika. Tomorrow is another day.

6

Awakened by two squirrels chattering loudly close to camp, I hear a wood thrush singing in the distance next. Then I hear the call of a loon echoing across the lake. I slept well last night thanks to chilly temps. What day is this? Oh yeah, Wednesday, my third day in the woods. Matika gets in my face right away. She lets me know that her pan is empty so I get up and fill it with water. She slops water all over the shelter floor as she drinks. That's it. We need a designated place for her pan – a place on the ground and out of the way. I move it to a slightly elevated spot near the front corner of the shelter. There. Now what was I doing? Time to drop the food bags and get breakfast going.

The sky overhead is cloudless this morning. A thin mist rolls over the glassy lake. I tramp down a partially overgrown beaver trail to the right of the shelter in order to reach the water's edge. There I snap a photo of the lake before doing anything else. I notice a large, brand new spider's web stretched between two tree branches on the way back to camp. Spiders are not my favorite creatures but I can't help admiring their work. The web is so beautiful shimmering in the sunlight, so orderly, so symmetrical. When did spiders learn how to do such remarkable work? How many millions of years ago? What precipitated it?

I pull out the camp stove and boil up water before feeding Matika and myself. I fix hot chocolate instead of tea for a change. Then I eat my usual bowl of granola. Matika gets the same old kibble, day after day, but never complains. She's big on smell but not very discriminating when it comes to taste. That's one of the advantages of being a dog, I suppose.

After breakfast, I make my way down to the lake's edge to pump water. As I go about this task, I spot newts swimming around less than a foot from shore. "C'mon in, the water's fine!" they seem to say. I might do just that later on. I have nothing planned today but thinking and writing. Collect some more wood perhaps. What else?

Back in camp, I pull out my cell phone – the fancy timepiece, that is. I'm tempted to see what time it is but quickly change my mind. The sun now shining brightly just above the trees tells me that it's roughly 8 or 9 o'clock in the morning. Beyond that it doesn't really matter. I putter about camp as if I have all the time in the world.

Time to get some more wood. I hike out to the main trail, passing shinleaf in bloom along the way. Its small white petals would be easy to miss, but I'm in tune with my surroundings this morning. Soon I find a huge downed tree with dead branches sticking up. This one is even better than the two I found yesterday. I start breaking off sticks, piling them at my feet. The branches snap crisply. The bark twists off easily. This is good wood for burning. As I go about this task, I notice all the activity taking place along the trunk: three kinds of fungus, two kinds of moss, and plenty of lichen are all doing their part to break down this tree. Insects are doing a job on it as well, and I can only imagine how many microbes are hard at work.

The forest engine. The cycle of life. I see a dynamic system all around me. "Nothing in wilderness escapes the universal interdependence," John Hay wrote in his book, *The Immortal Wilderness*. And here it is, humming right along. The forest floor is thick with all kinds of plants, both living and dead. Earthworms, beetles and god-knows-what are breaking down the detritus. A mosquito lands on my arm and I wonder how many more there are out here on the hunt. Probably best if I don't know. But the blood they extract from me and every other forest creature feeds the forest engine. It's all connected, yet no one player is indispensible. Not even me. Here it is: the web of life going full bore as it has for eons – long before that other web, the Internet, came along. Yet nature operates much the same way. Take out a chunk of it and the forest engine still hums along. Any vacancy doesn't last long. Everywhere I look there is growth and decay. It boggles the mind.

Back in camp once again, I pull out my field journal to record my thoughts. Matika gets in my face. After a day's rest she's feeling spry. She wants an adventure, but I think I'll wait another day before hiking over to Whitney Lake. Right now I have other things on my mind.

A strong wind blows in a few clouds. Is heavy weather afoot? Hard to say from this perspective, from a shelter perched on a small rise overlooking a wilderness lake. I have no way of knowing what the weather forecasters are saying. Whatever. All will be revealed in due time.

Is there any sound wilder than the call of a loon? Just now one sings its haunting song from the middle of the lake. Whenever I hear it, I surrender to absolute immediacy. My thoughts uncouple then disperse like an early morning mist, leaving me mesmerized by something unspeakable, by something out here that is utterly sublime. Than I snap out of it, returning to a more rational frame of mind. "It's only a bird call," I tell myself. But in my heart I know that isn't true.

I'm no naturalist. Not really. If I were I'd know the names of all the birds flying overhead, all the creatures around me, and all the plants on full display. More importantly, I would know how they interact with each other. But my knowledge of such things is sketchy, piecemeal, picked up here and there through the years. Some of it has been forgotten. Some things I will never know. If I were a naturalist, a true believer in the efficacy of wildness, I would sing nature's praises incessantly and curse my fellow man for despoiling it. But I am not comfortable separating humankind into *us* versus *them* – "us" being nature lovers, and "them" being those who just don't give a damn. I think it's more complicated than that. Humankind is "we" as far as I'm concerned, and that quickly becomes "I" whenever I start thinking long and hard about things. In other words, I take a good look at myself before pointing the finger at anyone else. Then I generalize to humankind as a whole the very shortcomings that I find within. And why not? Am I not utterly human? Am I not a perfect example of what is both right and wrong about my kind?

I stand in the middle of the wild and ask: "Who/what am I?" as if the label "human being" isn't enough of an answer. I want to know precisely what it means to be *Homo sapiens*, and how a brainy creature fits into the greater scheme of things. That is, how do I fit into it? "Man is a stream whose source is hidden," Ralph Waldo Emerson once wrote, but I venture deep into wildness looking for the source anyway. I want to understand the nature of myself as well as the world around me, and how they connect. This is a Herculean task, of course – one verging on absurdity. But I am not alone in this. There are thousands upon thousands of others doing the same right now, not to mention all those who have come before us. I am not the first person to harbor this powerful desire to know myself, nor will I be the last. Philosophers, poets, scientists, and theologians – all sorts of people come at this mystery from many different angles. There are countless books on the subject. Then there are direct encounters – those like me trying to experience the wild firsthand and extrapolate from that a deeper understanding of the human condition. Is it all for nothing?

What is it that's absolutely true about my human-ness? What separates man from myth? "The animality of man we can grasp with a fair degree of clarity," the theologian Abraham Heschel declared, "The perplexity begins when we attempt to make clear what is meant by the *humanity* of man." Amen to that, brother. When I look in the mirror, I see something of a stranger. I do not know myself completely, nor do I know exactly what it means to be human. If I did then I would know beyond all doubt how I fit into the greater scheme of things.

The one thing I do know is that I love being out here. I am drawn to the wild and feel at home in it. I consider what Emerson once wrote: "We can love nothing but nature." That makes me scratch my head. I think I know what he meant by that, and agree with it in principle, but am not sure that every other person on this planet would agree. The "we" that Emerson speaks about could easily be him, many others and me, but is it true of everyone? Emerson suggests that nature is all that is real, and we can only love what is real. But are there not those who love their illusions? Doesn't that count? If we don't know the difference between what is real and what is illusory, how can we truly love anything?

Again I must admit that I'm no naturalist. I don't know beyond all doubt the nature of things – especially human beings. That is, I don't know my own nature. Not completely. I remain a mystery to myself. And that unknowing must be extended to the world at large no matter how many birds, animals, or plants I can name, or how well I think I know their natures. It's a vicious circle. Without absolute knowledge of *self*, there can't be absolute knowledge of *other*... or vice versa.

The wind has been blowing steadily for some time now. I just caught a chill. That means it's a perfect day for a hike. Matika is ready to go. I pull out my fancy timepiece and check it. 11 o'clock. There's plenty of time left in the day to hike over to Whitney Lake and back. So then, let's do it!

7

After taking down the food bags, I set aside trail mix, two energy bars, and a serving of kibble. Then I consolidate all remaining food into one bag, emptying the other. The former goes back into the air. The latter becomes my daypack for the hike this afternoon since I didn't have the foresight to bring one on this trip. Some Boy Scout I am. Into the empty bag goes the food I've set aside, a wool shirt, my field journal, a topographical map, the water pump, and a liter of water. I sling the bag over my shoulder while holding its drawstring tightly. Then I grab one of my hiking poles and head out. Matika, dancing around me all the while, is right on my heels.

I take a right after walking out to the main trail. That's west-southwest according to my compass. I don't go far before that flooded section of trail next to the beaver pond appears. Traversing it isn't so bad – about twenty feet of sloshing through foot-deep mud and water. I'm able to hop between strategically placed puncheon and clumps of grass a good part of the way. Matika gets wet but doesn't care. She's happy to be on the move again.

A few minutes past the beaver pond, we stumble upon a stream. There's a single board spanning it where a bridge used to be. That works for me but

Matika isn't steady enough on her feet to negotiate that narrow board. She wades across.

I hike another two-thirds of a mile before spotting an unmarked spur trail. I recognize it from another outing many years earlier. Since it rises sharply uphill before disappearing into the understory, I'm almost certain that it's the trail to Whitney Lake. Almost. I take out my topo map and study the contour lines carefully to confirm this. I use my compass to verify that the trail does in fact point due west. Then away I go.

The path underfoot is sketchy, looking more like a game trail than anything used on a regular basis by hikers. I lose it more than once. But the old, weathered saw cuts in downed trees along the way keep me on track for the most part. This trail goes somewhere. It goes over one hill then drops to a low spot before hugging the side of another hill, just as the dotted line on my map indicates. I ford a small stream exiting a very small beaver pond. Sure enough, the beaver pond is shown on my map as a clearing of sorts. A pond called Puddle Hole lies not far north, according to my map that is. Getting close. Half a mile later, the trail empties into a grassy clearing. Then Whitney Lake pops into view.

The grassy clearing is about thirty feet across. There's supposed to be a shelter here, but that structure is long gone. The charred wood in the stone fire pit at one end of the clearing indicates that backpackers still camp here. What used to a great view of the lake is partially blocked by a few spruce trees about ten feet high. Off to the right, the ground eases down to the stony edge of the lake. That's an excellent water access. Unfortunately, it's tainted by what looks like soap suds. Perhaps tannins in the water from decaying vegetation caused those suds. I'd like to think that's the case, anyhow.

The lake is bigger than expected, about half a mile across and considerably longer. It's shallow a long way out and crystal clear. Easy to make out its stony bottom. The nearly cloudless sky overhead gives the rippled surface of the lake a slightly bluish cast. Spruce trees line the lake's edge all the way around, with a heavily forested hill rising from the far shore. This is a beautiful place. I'd camp here if I had all my gear with me. Maybe I should go back and get it.

Still in scouting mode, I follow a trail peeling away to the left of the clearing. It fades beneath a thick copse of conifers. By the time I realize that the trail underfoot is gone, Matika and I are standing in a minefield of rusty old cans and broken glass bottles. An image of Matika's bleeding paws pops into my head. I grab hold of her by the collar and immediately back out of there. I spot a 50-gallon drum on the way out. Why someone used this place as a dump is beyond me. How all this crap got here is an even greater mystery. Whitney Lake is in the middle of a wilderness. Was all this trash flown in here before this became a designated wilderness area? That's my best guess. One thing is certain, though. Camping here with my dog is out of the question. Can't risk her stepping on something sharp.

I follow another trail to the right of the clearing, but not very far. It goes down to the small outlet stream of the nearby pond, Puddle Hole. Beyond the stream – forget about it. I don't see anything over there that looks even remotely like a trail. My topo map promises a trail extending north from here all the way to Cedar Lakes, several miles away, but I don't believe that for a second. The map is old, and the one thing I've learned while hiking in the Adirondacks through the decades is that unused trails become overgrown a lot faster than one might think.

Matika and I return to the grassy clearing then find a nice place to sit along the lake's edge. It's time for lunch. But first I do battle with the dozen or so deer flies that we picked up during our hike here. I kill half of them before the rest fly away.

Matika wolfs down her lunch in less than a minute. While slowly eating mine, I jot a few lines in my field journal, occasionally gazing dreamily across the lake. Water gently lapping to shore washes away all care. The wild commands my full attention. There's no room in my head for abstract thoughts right now. Just sky, trees, and water lapping endlessly to shore...

Back on the trail, retracing my steps. Whitney Lake was a nice diversion. Hiking to it was good exercise. Glad I made the effort, but I'm just as happy to be headed back to Pillsbury Lake. I wonder if anyone has shown up there in my absence. What will they think when they see my stuff in the shelter? I pushed it all to one side again before leaving, just in case someone wants to stay.

Upon reaching the stream close to Pillsbury Lake, I pump a bottle full of cold, clear water. I drink my fill of it in the process. Lake water works, but cold stream water is much better. Funny how something as basic as water can feel so good going down. It reminds me how much of an earthbound creature I still am despite all my abstractions.

As Matika and I negotiate the flooded spot next to the beaver pond that's close to camp, we spook a great blue heron. It spreads its wings then leaps into the air with remarkable grace. The pond impresses me, as well. It's only a small patch of still water reflecting the blue sky and surrounding vegetation. Not much when you think about it, yet alluring all the same. Is beauty only the wild emptying our minds of everything other than what is immediately before us? If that's the case, then both herons and beaver ponds are immeasurably beautiful.

Back in camp, I'm a little surprised to find my things exactly how I left them. There's no indication that anyone has come along in my absence. I'm still alone out here. Hmm, how strange... No matter how many times I experience deep woods solitude, I never quite get used to it.

I'm not that hungry but Matika gets another ration of kibble for her exertion. She sucks it right down. Then I clean her up the best I can. I wipe down her underside and remove all the sticks and leaf litter from her fur anyhow. Wilderness dog. Yeah, she's starting to look the part.

Time to clean up myself as well. With temps in the high 70s this afternoon, a dip in the lake seems like a good idea. I grab a small camp towel and head down to the lake's edge, past the first access to the one where I don't draw my drinking water. Off come my clothes. The aquatic vegetation is thick around the second water access, but the lake bottom drops away fast enough for me to take the plunge after wading only a few feet from shore. Matika stays on high dry ground, in no mood to get any wetter than she already is. I swim out far enough to feel the cool caress of deeper waters. I swim in broad circles, kicking my feet free of any strands of vegetation below, as three days of dirt and sweat wash away. Then I return to shore.

After checking myself for leeches, I stand on the lake's edge for a moment or two, dripping dry. With closed eyes raised to the midsummer sun, I enjoy its warmth against my skin. I am a denizen of this wild world, as much at home here as any other creature. My body is more than just a vessel for abstract thoughts, or a temporary home for the so-called spiritual self. It is a big part of who/what I am. In fact, I wonder if any semblance of this thing called "I" can exist without it. No matter. While toweling myself off, I revel in my *physical* existence. The rest is beyond me right now. Strangely enough, I feel a tinge of sadness while putting my clothes back on. I'm a little unsteady on my feet in the process. A good part of my youthful vitality has dissipated through the years, leaving me all too aware that I will not live forever.

8

Late afternoon, or is it evening? It doesn't matter. I'm feeling very relaxed right now. Matika and I went under the net for a long nap after getting cleaned up. Now here we are ready for whatever's next. Glad I hiked over to Whitney Lake. That seemed to work out any remaining concern I had about anything, although the word "concern" might not be appropriate here. "Anxiety" isn't the right word, either, because I haven't felt that since I landed in this shelter. What then? Concern in a different sense, perhaps – for the human condition? No, that's an abstract concern so it's not pressing. Concern for my own well being? No, I'm not feeling that – not right now, anyhow. I'm feeling good.

Is this what happiness feels like? I usually don't think about it. In my life back in the developed lowlands, I'm too busy trying to complete tasks and achieve modest goals to dwell upon how I'm feeling. My work makes me happy, I suppose. No, it makes me more than happy. I am satisfied most days. I am satisfied with my work, my marriage, with life in general. I think more about money matters than I'd like to, but that's because it always seems to be in short supply. That said, I usually have enough money to get by. Back in 2012, I faced up to a harsh reality: my inability to make a living by writing alone. It was a depressing realization, certainly, but I'm over that now. Have been for some time. Since abandoning the dream of making a living by writing alone, I've been able to think and write more about philosophical matters – philosophy being just about as far away from the literary marketplace as one can get. It has been a rather ironic liberation. After all, the urge to philosophize is why I became a writer in the first place.

Satisfaction, dissatisfaction. If I were to change anything in my life, I would spend more time with family and friends. Doing more things with my wife Judy – that's always at the top of my want list – but spending time with others is another big desire. Siblings, aged parents, stepsons, grandkids, and friends both old and new – I miss them all. I never get enough time with them. That's a funny thing to say while camped alone in the wild for days on end, but there you have it. One values most what can't be taken for granted.

A pair of loons call back and forth across the lake. I spot one of them close by. The other is much farther away, somewhere out of sight. Magnificent sounds! Such a beautiful duet. So utterly enchanting. I could sit here and listen to them all day.

I'm hungry but in no mood to eat. That is, I'm enjoying a hungry happiness. It's a sensation I've often experienced while alone in deep woods. Back in the developed lowlands, I am simply hungry. But out here it's a different story. There's something good about not eating when there's an adequate cache of food nearby. This could also be true in developed places, I suppose, but in wild places being hungry seems more immediate – a strangely pleasant validation of one's animal self. As long as there's food to be had, of course.

I'm starting to miss Judy, but not enough to leave this place. Wish I could share this beautiful lake with her or someone else. That's the problem with solitary adventures. They are, well, solitary. Introduce another person and everything changes. I once went into the woods with a close friend, and we agreed to spend a chunk of one day apart – each of us going our own way. But even then, a sense of the other person's presence went away. Alone in deep woods that *human* otherness doesn't exist. Alone in deep woods, there is only self and the wild. And after a while the line between the two begins to blur.

I have my dog Matika with me, of course. That's all the companionship I need right now. Funny thing about canine companions: they can be right by one's side without compromising the slow and steady immersion into the wild that one undergoes out here. Our interspecies relationship doesn't change this process. Go figure.

For better or worse, two human beings together create a society for themselves wherever they go. It's usually for the better, but something is always lost as a result. To immerse oneself completely in the wild, one has to go alone into it. This is a no-no, of course, as far as the managers of public spaces and other officials are concerned. It's much easier to get into trouble when you're alone in the wild, and much harder to deal with trouble when it comes. But that's a risk I have always been willing to take. Some think such risk-taking is selfish because I might need to be rescued someday. A rescue mission costs a lot of money, ties up valuable resources, and sometimes endangers those doing the rescuing. In response to this I say: don't come looking for me then. Where's the waiver? I'll sign it. Let me die out here if it comes to that, and let the wild pick my bones clean.

Every excursion alone into the wild is a spiritual undertaking of sorts. That's how it feels to me, anyhow. God, or the "Eternal Thou" as the theologian Martin Buber called it, is manifest in nature. Of that I am certain. And, as Buber says: "The primary word I-Thou can be spoken only with the whole being." In other words, a bona fide relationship between one being and another is always unqualified, uncompromised, soul-to-soul. Perhaps that is why I have been so reluctant over the years to come out here and just sit, giving wild nature my undivided attention. As I learned in the Alaskan bush back in '92, that kind of relationship can be overwhelming. At least while I'm hiking a trail there are brief encounters with other hikers to soften the intensity of wildness, to give me a break from the Eternal Thou. Who can gaze unblinkingly into the face of God for long without turning into stone?

The gentle breeze that has been blowing all day just stopped. The sky has clouded over. Is a storm imminent? All my gear is tucked into a corner of the shelter so it makes little difference to me. But I'm thinking I should fire up my camp stove and eat dinner before any rain comes down. Besides, I'm really hungry now. The happiness in it has gone away.

Dinner is another dehydrated meal – beef stroganoff – reconstituted with boiling water. The wind picks up while I'm eating. It clears out the clouds. Funny how in tune with the weather I am out here, how no change in it goes unnoticed. Can't remember when I have lived this much in the present. Probably the last time I spent a day or two just hanging out in the woods.

After dinner I sling a single food bag back into the air, acutely aware that I'm halfway through my time out here. Don't need to check my fancy timepiece to know that. The food supply diminishes as time passes. When it's gone, it'll be time to return to the developed lowlands.

The sun is low in the sky now, just off the southwestern shoulder of Noisey Ridge. Third evening alone. No one has come along yet. How strange.

The bugs come out in force when the wind stops. I build a small fire to keep them at bay. Actually, I build a small fire just because I can. It's something to do while watching the sun set. Orange flames dance in the center of the fire pit, consuming the sticks that I place there – one right after another. The fire burns clean, without smoke. Then comes the pink afterglow in the distance, beyond a dark silhouette of trees. A cloudless evening. Still air. Still lake. And all's quiet except the crackling of a fire. Twilight. Almost ready to go to bed. Almost. The bugs will ultimately drive me under the net.

9

Another quiet, perfectly still morning. A few wispy clouds overhead reflect the early light. Heavy dew has collected in the patches of grass around the shelter. Comfortable temps right now. That means it's going to be a warm day – a day for slathering on the bug dope that is.

Rough night last night. It was a little too warm to sleep for one thing. Mosquitoes whining at the net didn't help matters. Matika stretched out at one point, creating an opening in the net that those little buggers exploited. I woke up in the middle of the night and killed several blood-engorged mosquitoes as a consequence. I wanted to bark "Bad dog!" at Matika, but wasn't sure that she fully understands the mosquito net concept. So I manhandled her body back under the net, gave her a few snugs, then tried to get back to sleep.

Oh yeah, I'm feeling every one of my 61 years this morning as I get up and start moving around. Glad to be here all the same. Looking forward to doing a lot of nothing today, entertaining whatever thoughts come my way. Will keep my camera handy. Will keep the binoculars handy as well. Never know what's going to show up.

I fire up the camp stove then place a small covered pot full of water on it. Soon the lid is dancing atop bubbles as the water boils. How much of animation in the world is only the dynamics of heat and water? Is that all there is to life forms? Are we nothing more than chemistry? Those are pretty heavy questions to ask before the first cup of tea in the morning, but I can't help myself. I'm a philosopher more by temperament than choice.

My usual bowl of granola for breakfast then I'll open up my journal and start writing. Philosophy fueled by granola, hmm… Some people would scoff at that. Perhaps I should ponder the nature of the universe on an empty stomach. Perhaps I should toss the journal aside and meditate in a half-lotus position instead. No doubt how we approach matters of ultimate concern determines the conclusions that we draw.

A sparrow flits into camp – the one that has been serenading me with its five-note song each morning. I raise my binoculars to see a streak of yellow trailing away from its eye. Will be sure to look it up in my bird identification book when I get home, but right now I'm comfortable calling it a song sparrow. After all, that's what it does. I quick draw my binoculars as another songbird flies into camp. Ah, too slow. Better luck next time.

The spider's web that I found near camp yesterday is best seen from an angle. Head on, it virtually disappears. So it is with any approach to Nature – nature with a capital "N" that is, the ultimate concern of philosophers. The scientist breaks the natural world down into particulars. When a philosopher does this, Nature disappears, leaving one to conclude that the whole is merely the sum of its parts. But with a sidelong glance a nearly invisible web reappears – the structure that holds all things together.

Philosophy is primarily concerned with the structure of the universe. That is why most people have no time for it. They don't believe that such a structure really exists. Or if it does, then surely it has been fashioned by God so it is beyond our comprehension. After all, who can know what God is up to? No one can, of course, so why bother looking?

As philosophers some of us can't help but look. And when we are lucky enough, the web appears briefly as we are pondering things. But when we look at it head on, trying to systematize what we see into some kind of *–Ism*, it disappears again. The sidelong glance is all we have.

How can we really know Nature? "The hidden shows up in too-plain sight," the writer Annie Dillard tells us, "It lives captive on the face of the obvious." If that is true then all I need to know about Nature is right in front of me. The trick, of course, is to decipher the obvious, to find universal truth in the simplest things. That's precisely what I've been trying to do for decades, both in my study at home and here in the wild. And yet I still can't say that I know Nature. It remains the first, the last, the greatest mystery of them all.

What is truth? We can't say with absolute certainty what is true about the world and what is not, so let's forget about it. Let's step away from this unsolvable puzzle called Nature and go get a beer. Hmm... I like drinking beer as much as the next guy, but I'd skip that if doing so would give me a better shot at the truth. "God offers every mind its choice between truth and repose," Ralph Waldo Emerson once said. That was rather presumptuous of him, wasn't it? Just because we seek truth, doesn't mean we will obtain it. One questions whether or not it's even possible to obtain truth. Truth is, by definition, absolute. The truth of the world is the *whole* truth and nothing else. Is the human mind even capable of comprehending the whole? Perhaps going for a beer is the better choice.

We are in the bad habit of looking for truth in books – in scientific writings, rational treatises, or sacred scriptures. But all these things are manmade, which is to say derivative. What is real is right in front of us each and every day. Our wordy abstractions veil the concrete. Oddly enough, it takes a little imagination for a human being to see what is obvious to every other creature on the planet. Our preconceptions about the world keep getting in the way.

"Nature teaches more than she preaches," John Burroughs wrote, "There are no sermons in stones." That says it all. We desire divine revelation but find only stony truths. If we are really paying attention, that is.

A sparrow hops across the woodpile. Two chipmunks sneak into camp. I throw nuts to them all. That is, while Matika snoozes, I fraternize with the enemy, letting wild nature encroach. Uh-oh, Matika just woke up. I toss a biscuit her way to distract her, but my canine companion is not so easily fooled. She scrambles to her feet and chases away the bird and chipmunks. Then she pees along the edge of camp, drawing her line in the sand. A squirrel approaches a few minutes later. A toad creeps into view. Suddenly there are butterflies everywhere. "You're losing control!" I shout at Matika while bursting into laughter.

Just now a sparrow hops into the fire pit. That's where I dump my dishwater. Surely the sparrow is finding tiny bits of food there. Food is everything – the fuel that keeps us all going…

Reproduction, ingestion, growth. What is it all for? Sometimes I think that it's all *for* nothing. Life just *is*. But that doesn't explain why life forms came into being in the first place. Okay, the universe sprang from a singularity, morphed into superhot plasma, then into stars and galaxies. That much makes sense from a strictly materialistic standpoint. Inorganic chemistry makes sense. But why life? What need was there for the inanimate to become animate? In a strictly material universe, what need was there for living things? They seem superfluous. In a world dominated by fire, water and stone, as our world was a billion years ago, the emergence of life forms seem so freakish, unnatural.

The basic concept of evolution is easy enough to understand, but it leaves so much unexplained. First and foremost, why is there evolution instead of utter chaos? Things evolve randomly we are told, but why do they evolve at all? To what end? Pull this string long enough and the materialistic worldview unravels. Why is anything organized? Why have stars coalesced into galaxies? Why are some galaxies spiral and others spherical, while still others are disorganized? Why gravity? Why the so-called laws of physics?

"Organization demands an organizing principle," John Burroughs concluded after pondering this matter, and I wholeheartedly agree. That is why Burroughs, me, and like-minded others call ourselves pantheists, however reluctantly. In a dynamic universe, one that is clearly as organized as ours, there is plenty of room for chaos, for random acts, but that isn't the be–all and end-all of existence. Nature is more than just a convenient label for everything that has arisen by pure chance from nothingness. Nature *exists* apart from our mere idea of it, or at least that is what some of us believe. It is divine, which is to say that something is organizing it. What that something is, well, that's anyone's guess.

"Life is inexpressible," the effervescent thinker John Brockman wrote, "Life is inexcusable." I assume that he was referring to his own life when he wrote that, but it describes life in general just as well. A billion years ago there was absolutely no reason for it – not one that I can see, anyhow. Stones were enough. The physical universe did not need to evolve beyond that. No, it didn't even need to go that far. The stones themselves imply a complex set of physical laws that we take for granted. The existence of *anything* is inexcusable. Is the periodic table the consequence of an utterly random universe? I think not. Are the basic forces of the universe a foregone conclusion after the toss of cosmic dice?   Surely you jest!

Reason has its limitations.   All logical arguments become circular.   They are always rooted in givens that are not really given.   We assume too much and our thoughts derail as a consequence.   It can't be helped. There is no way to think concretely.   There is no way to ponder the physical without slipping into the meta-physical.

Evolution, what a concept.   I'm convinced that it's the key to understanding the true miracle of the universe – what Nature is all about.   I'm convinced that evolution is the only proof there is of the existence of God. Evolution shouts organization.   To what end, God only knows.   But there it is, hidden in plain sight.

God.   That confounding word!   "'God' is the most heavy-laden of all human words," Martin Buber declared, "None has become so soiled, so mutilated. Just for this reason I may not abandon it."   My sentiment exactly.   I won't abandon it either, despite its baggage, because there's no point discussing the organization of Nature without it.   Chance plays a role in the evolution of things, no doubt, but what's the impetus?   The French philosopher Henri Bergson was the first Darwinian philosopher to give this question serious consideration.   "Life transcends finality as it transcends other categories," he wrote. "It is essentially a current sent through matter, drawing from it what it can."   *Élan vital*, he called it – the vital force.   Say what we will about the absurdly mystical qualities this worldview, it makes more sense than philosophical materialism. Causation lies at the root of evolution, of course. Without causation, evolution can't happen – it lacks impetus. And wherever there is impetus, there is divinity. In other words, natural order really does exist. The laws of nature are not just figments of our collective imagination.

While bushwhacking through the forest, I am well aware of the woody chaos all around me. But when I look closely, I see whorled leaves, intricate patterns in wildflowers, symmetry. Then I hear birdsongs. Yet there is randomness at work in this wild world as well. The wind blows every which way. Trees fall down and all kinds of things happen, both expected and unexpected. Growth and decay. Nature is the dance of order and chaos. It's all here, in the wild landscape before me.

A float plane passes overhead, reminding me of my brief sojourn in the Alaskan bush decades ago, and the feeling back then of being detached temporarily from the rest of humanity. Day four here at Pillsbury Lake, and I still haven't seen anyone. Not that I'm complaining.

Why philosophize? What purpose does it serve? No roads or houses have ever been built by it. No fields are ever cultivated by these cerebral efforts. Philosophizing is an utterly useless undertaking. Yet the Taoist sage Chuang Tzu said, "Only those who already know the value of the useless can be talked to about the useful."

Just now a butterfly lands on my leg. Hard to say whether it is validating my thoughts or mocking them. But one thing is for certain: I have arrived. I came out here to cast my abstractions into the wild and see how they fare. The butterfly renders its verdict. I, *Homo sapiens*, am a thinking creature, and there is something very strange about that. Nature does not need my thinking. It was doing just fine before I came along. And yet, and yet...

Matika rests at my feet, not thinking much at all. The butterfly flutters away then returns to land on me again. A wild creature, a domesticated dog and me. It's quite the combination, really, undermining all comfortable notions about self and other, about civilization and wildness. Where are the clear boundaries between such things? Wild nature encroaches, both physically and mentally. If I sit here long enough, it will swallow me whole.

10

While stepping away from my field journal for a while, I take a good look at the vegetation around the shelter. Most of the trees are red spruce, balsam fir, or paper birches. Beneath them grows striped maple, some kind of berry bush, a tall plant with clusters of tiny white flowers, some kind of buttercup, and several other large plants that I can't identify. Frustrating. I don't know half of it. But the plants growing closer to the ground look very familiar: the blue beads arising from yellow clintonia, the browned leaves of lilies, and bunchberry gone to seed. There's sedge grass and plantain along the beaten paths, of course, and lichen clinging to trees both living and dead. And moss everywhere.

Moss, hmm… Tardigrades love moss. I can't see moss now without thinking about them. The day before I left the house for these woods, my wife Judy brought to my attention an article about this curious little creature. A tardigrade is more affectionately called a water bear, even though it looks nothing like any animal I've ever seen before, let alone a bear. With eight stumpy legs and a segmented body, this microscopic creature is positively alien looking, as are most life forms that are too small for the naked eye to see. And it *is* alien to us to some extent, with traits unlike any other creature we know. Tardigrades can live decades without food or water, existing in a state of dehydration that would kill any other animal. Here is a multicellular creature over 500 million years old that can survive intense heat or cold, radiation, severe droughts, and even the vacuum of space. They've been found everywhere on the planet, from the summits of mountains to deep-sea volcanoes, from tropical rain forests to the Antarctic. And they love moss. There are probably a bunch of them around me right now.

Tardigrades are evolutionary overkill, if you ask me. Then again, they are a guarantee that life will continue in some form on this planet despite the worst that we do to it. Here or elsewhere in the universe, tardigrades or creatures like them will persist long after we are gone. That certainly makes one think twice before declaring *Homo sapiens* the pinnacle of evolution. We are an evolutionary dead end compared to these tough little guys.

To the naked eye, it seems there are more insects than any other creatures on this planet. Yet microscopic creatures like tardigrades abound. Then there is vegetation. Surely there are more plants than animals in terms of the sheer planetary biomass. And yet bacteria – those original life forms – are virtually everywhere, and God only knows how much of that exists. So what is it then? What's the dominant life form on planet Earth? Does this world belong to insects, microscopic creatures, vegetation, or bacteria? Not mammals, that's for sure. Not us. We are an evolutionary afterthought. We can trash this world, it seems, but we can't own it.

Time to clean up Matika a bit. I comb her out, removing all the leaves, sticks and other forest detritus from her fur. I take a few knots out of her fur as well, though the worst of it Judy will have to deal with later. Judy did a great job grooming Matika before we came out here so she still looks good for the most part. I'm simply doing what I can to keep her from looking feral.

After the grooming session, I apply Skin So Soft repellent to Matika to keep the bugs at bay. Now she smells pretty. Then I slather some 100% deet on myself. I hate bug dope – especially the toxic smell of it. But when the bugs are as thick as they are right now, one has to do something.

Checking my fancy timepiece, I'm surprised to see that it's noon already. I've geared waaay down. I've spent an entire morning with squirrels, sparrows, butterflies, chipmunks and my ruminations. And I haven't ventured more than fifty yards away from the shelter since I got out of bed.

An inchworm floats down slowly from the shelter roof, dangling by a nearly invisible strand of silk. It lands on my finger. What kind of beetle is that – long, brown and flying into camp just now? Frogs croak along the water's edge, 24/7. A cedar waxwing suddenly appears. The sky is cloudy right now, all grey and white with very little definition. Nearby a wood thrush sings its enchanting flute-like song, over and over, convincing me that I'm right were I should be.

I didn't think much of Pillsbury Lake when I first landed here, but it's growing on me. Islands, nearby hills, a sprawling shoreline – this is a beautiful place. And the shelter is in just the right spot. Too bad the bees own the best access to the water. Too bad trees obstruct the view from the shelter. But those are minor inconveniences. This is an utterly wild place surrounded by forest and populated by loons. That's all that matters.

Sometimes I find it difficult to sit quiet and still, entertaining my thoughts while immersed in wildness. My mind recoils from it, afraid of what might exist beneath the surface of my own seemingly gentle nature. A part of me is afraid of the wildness that stirs deep within. It's a primal fear to be sure – a deep-seated fear of the unknown that we all have. We are afraid, first and foremost, of what we were *before* we became civilized. We imagine the worst – evil being rooted, presumably, in our savage selves. But letting go of that, it becomes incredibly easy to simply live in the moment, sinking into the natural world and allowing one's wildness to surface. A butterfly lands on me and suddenly I am nothing more than a perch. That compels me to laugh at the absurdity of my exalted self-image: I, *Homo sapiens*, the be-all and end-all of existence! The know-it-all animal! A godlike creature! Nature encroaches upon my tidy camp, making hash of my ridiculous sense of self-importance. Slowly, as wildness recaptures my heart and mind, all my carefully constructed preconceptions about the world and myself come into question. All of them.

The wind whispers a secret across the lake and through the trees. I listen carefully, but can't quite make it out. Its secret remains a secret.

Humankind has a tendency to organize things, to put them in boxes, in categories. I am no exception to this. I talk about my body, mind and soul as if they are separate things. I ponder the relationships between God, humankind and nature as if they aren't inextricably entwined. We assume that the physical and spiritual are two entirely different realms, and that's how our thoughts become muddled. "Spirit and life are complimentary and interrelated," the German philosopher Max Scheler wrote, and we nod our heads in agreement. Yet we still keep things in boxes. This is only natural, I suppose. The rational mind – the mind of *Homo sapiens*, that is – wants to make sense of everything, to organize the world, and put everything in its place. Reason is a tool that has served us well through the millennia. Why stop now? So into boxes everything goes. But that's no way to comprehend the world as a whole. To do that, we must see the most important connection, the fundamental relationship between what is seen and what is unseen.

Does Nature will itself? Is the apparent order that we see in the natural world an extension of the *mind* of Nature? Clearly more is unknown than known to us whenever we go down this path, but how can we avoid doing so? There is no other way to comprehend the world as a whole. Without some idea what Nature is all about, our understanding of the world in general, or our selves in particular, is piecemeal. So we must at least try.

What is the magic in the machine, the essence behind existence itself – that which lies beyond the parts and thereby constitutes the whole? Nature is the great mystery. Nature with a capital "N" that is. The study of its parts is science; the study of the whole is philosophy. Understanding it requires an abstract thinker, not a technician, and a damned good one at that. What we need is a dynamic philosophy – one that doesn't settle on any given *-Ism* then call it a day. What is required here is a rigorous philosophy that questions everything, even the context in which the questions are raised. Even then, comprehending the whole may forever elude us. After all, we do like our boxes.

"How natural is natural," the renowned essayist and anthropologist Loren Eiseley once asked, "And is there anything we can call a natural world at all?" When I first read this, I scoffed. Of course there's a natural world. That's obvious to anyone who has eyes to see, ears to hear, and fingers to touch. But our understanding of it is inadequate, piecemeal, reductionist. This, I think, is what Eiseley was driving at. There are so many worlds, so many possibilities.

There are countless ways to fashion a molecule, to organize matter. There are an infinite number of permutations it seems – ways that energy can be organized into physical things. We mess around in our laboratories and out comes something artificial. Or is it? What chemical compound can we invent that doesn't already exist in nature? If all things artificial are also natural phenomenon to some extent, does this thing called nature even exist? It's a troubling thought, but one that we should entertain all the same.

In Nature all things are possible. This is what evolution teaches us. So what is "natural" but a set of assumptions we make about the world? Is anything truly un-natural? Better yet, does Nature exist apart from some romantic notion we have of it? It seems heretical to ask questions like these while immersed in the wild, yet they are critical questions all the same.

I claim to love nature, but do I really love all of it? Perhaps I am a romantic, more in love with the idea of nature than nature itself. I love sunsets and songbirds, beautiful wildflowers, wild animals that rarely appear, misty mountains, clear streams, and quiet ponds. I love trails winding deep into the forest. But I must admit there are times when I am absolutely miserable out here: hypothermic or overheated, bug-bitten, wet, dirty, exhausted, disoriented or afraid. As Gary Snyder says: "Life in the wild is not just eating berries in the sunlight." There is a harsh side to nature that shows itself every time a terrible storm takes place, or something else threatens us. I do not love hurricanes or diseases, blood-sucking creatures or droughts. Who does? My beloved nature is always ideal. The wilderness I cavort through is only marginally threatening. And always there is a way out – a path leading back to the developed lowlands where food is abundant and comfort is commonplace. What then makes my frolics in the wild any different from the silliness of some reality TV show?

No one has ever romanticized starvation. Keeping that at bay is the primary object of civilization. That's food for thought, indeed. Something for me to ponder between meals, as my food supply slowly runs out.

What is Nature really? It's something for philosophers to ponder. It's the ultimate abstraction – the concrete turned abstract. But to ponder such things is a luxury. There's no point posing this question to someone who is starving to death. It would immediately be dismissed as irrelevant.

Hmm... Looks like a storm is brewing. The western sky is ominous. There's a dark grey cloud mass headed this way. And all the bugs have mysteriously disappeared. I'd better go pump some more water and put all my things under cover before it rains.

11

A gentle rain falls as Matika and I get up from a late afternoon nap. The wind gusts occasionally, sending a chill right through me. I put on my rain jacket to stay warm. My woodpile is covered with a plastic bag that's held down by a heavy metal grate that I pulled out of the fire pit when I first landed here. Everything else is stashed in the shelter and dry. So let the rain do its thing. It keeps the bugs down.

Day four and still alone. Hard to believe that I'll have this shelter all to myself for another night. Then again, few hikers come out when it's raining. I've corralled all my gear into the left half of the shelter just in case.

As the rain subsides, a bold chipmunk scurries into the fire pit. Then it inches closer to us. Matika crouches on the outside edge of the shelter floor, watching it intently. When the chipmunk draws a little closer, she bolts after it. All I can do is laugh while settling into my favorite spot against the shelter wall and pulling out my journal.

This incredible universe, the miracle of life, the great mystery of nature, and the myriad complexities and contradictions of being human – it all presses reason to its limits and beyond. I call myself a philosopher but there are times when the word "mystic" seems more appropriate. I ponder the imponderable. When pressed to it, I cannot fully explain Nature. I can only gaze upon it and marvel. I see nothing in Nature but paradoxes. There are too many questions that can't be answered. Even with the vast amount of knowledge that we have accumulated over the centuries, there are still too many unknowns. In fact, the more we learn, the more questions arise, and the greater a mystery Nature becomes. The particulars are easy to analyze, organize and study. But Nature with a capital "N" – the driving force behind all existence – that's beyond us. No book I've cracked open during the past 45 years has illuminated me regarding that, anyhow. All I have is speculation. All any of us have is speculation. So I call myself a philosopher and plumb the depths of what is known about the world only to immerse myself in wildness like this every once in a while and be amazed.

A nature-loving philosopher/mystic? I'm not the first one to come along, that's for sure. There's a strong tradition of it here in America: Emerson, Thoreau and Burroughs to name a few. Embrace Nature and you can't help but become a philosopher/mystic to some extent. The wild is everywhere, all around us, deep within us. Yet it remains fundamentally unspeakable, mysterious.

In his book *Mysticism and Philosophy*, W. T. Stace says that mysticism "blatantly breeches the laws of logic at every turn," and that's how most people perceive it. But I don't think it's that easy. Yes, if you're talking simple "if P then Q" logic, then surely mysticism disappoints. But I believe that there is another way to think – a way to face the irreconcilable paradoxes of the world without having one's head explode. Our brains are not computers. They don't necessarily freeze up when confronted with conflicting statements. Paradox is precisely where philosophy and mysticism converge. That's where a different kind of knowledge emerges. Immanuel Kant called it *synthetic a priori*. Others call it intuition, though I think that's a little off the mark. As for me, well, I don't know what to call it. All I know is that there are moments, ecstatic moments, when I comprehend Nature in some wordless way, knowing in my gut something about it that is otherwise impossible to know. I *believe* this comprehension is rooted in reality, not illusion. But how can I be certain? I can't. After all, beliefs are entirely subjective.

What a difference an hour makes! It couldn't have been more than that since the rain was falling. Now the sky is blue as far as I can see. It's as if I was dreaming that it rained then suddenly awoke to a sunny day.

While fetching water for dinner, I splash a little of it into my face then raise my closed eyes to the sky before opening them to a brightly shining sun. It's a pagan prayer of sorts – a way of engaging the elemental world and saying thanks for it. I feel lucky to be alive.

It's hard not thinking about others, even when ensconced in wilderness solitude. My binoculars remind me of my brother Greg. He gave them to me many years back. I purchased my hunting knife and sleeping bag from friends long ago. A childhood friend, now deceased, gave me the tent poles that I use to set up my tarp. My mother gave me the Swiss Army knife that I've kept in my back pocket for decades. My map and compass remind me of my friend Steve, who is now a professional cartographer. The bug dope reminds me of my grandkids. I slather it on them every time I take them into the woods. The list goes on. I associate things with people. Does everyone do this? Even without things as reminders, is it ever possible to be completely alone? We carry our relationships with others everywhere we go.

According to my fancy timepiece, it's now a little past 7:30. It's safe to say I'll be spending another night alone here. Hard to believe. This is Thursday.

Tomorrow the weekend begins. Surely someone will show up then. Pillsbury Lake is only four miles from the trailhead and this is the middle of summer. Can't imagine I'll be alone here much longer.

Provision inventory time. After eating the last dehydrated meal, I spread the contents of my food bag across the shelter floor. There are plenty of energy bars left, only a few tea bags (of all things to be running low), two servings of breakfast cereal, another package of ramen noodles, and some trail mix. The beef jerky and jelly beans are long gone (of course), but there are plenty of treats for Matika. And kibble too. I have enough toilet paper but not what I'd call a surplus. Plenty of fuel for the stove, as well. Yeah, I can easily stay out here a couple more days.

Dusk. With lots of wood on hand, I build a small campfire. The first one I built was to keep up the skills. The one last night was for pleasure. This one is religion. Feeding, maintaining, and then working the fire down to embers is an elaborate ritual that I practice as the sky glows orange, then turns pink, then fades to darkness. The crackle and snap of the burning sticks clears my head. My thoughts become smoke. And, as the glowing embers cool, I become thankful for everything, everything.

Matika nestles against the shelter wall after we both slip beneath the mosquito net. How strange. She usually likes to be on the open side so that she can stretch out. But when she noses my arm, I get it. She wants some attention. I pet her. We do this at home, just before lights out, and she's always on my right side. I pet her while closing my eyes and listening to frogs croaking endlessly. Soon we are both down for the count.

12

A bright light suddenly shines in my face, quickly followed by a second one. "Whoa!" I shout, bolting straight up from my resting place. Matika does the same. I was almost asleep so it takes a moment to process what's happening. Two young men are now standing in front of the shelter, asking if there's a good place here to camp. "Not really," I say. Then I invite them into the shelter. They say they don't want to impose. I'm thinking it's too late for that.

They tell me their names: Todd and Phil. I tell them mine. The three of us stand in front of the shelter while getting acquainted – me in my underwear. Matika walks over to give both of the newcomers a good sniffing. They stand perfectly still, each holding out a friendly hand. They seem to know dogs. Matika assures me that they're okay.

It's ten o'clock. They apologize for coming in so late. Their car had a flat tire on the way here. Todd asks again if there are any good camping spots nearby, and again I invite them into the shelter. But no, that won't work. They plan on staying up a while longer this evening drinking whiskey and don't want to keep me awake. They consider camping on the grassy spot next to the shelter, right in front of the trail to the nearest water access. That's when I warn them about the nest of bees down there. Good thing I do. Phil is allergic to bees. Pointing to the left, I tell them that there are a couple sketchy places to camp about fifty yards away. Todd checks out those places while Phil gets to know Matika and me a little better.

Phil says they're out for three days. They're hiking the loop from here to West Lake then over to Cedar Lakes, then back to the trailhead. They plan on sleeping in tomorrow so they'll be getting a late start. That's another reason they don't want to come into the shelter. They figure I'll be up and moving about early. They're right about that.

When Todd comes back, he announces that he found a good spot to pitch their tent. This surprises me so I ask where. Todd says it's right next to the lake. Hmm... that's my water access. I'll have to be real quiet when I go down for water in the morning. They invite me to join them for a little whiskey. I politely decline, suggesting that they come visit me in the morning when they get up. They agree to that, shoulder their packs then walk away.

Beneath the net again, I try to get back to sleep but that's not happening. My mind is racing. I have company now and that changes everything. Todd and Phil seem nice enough. They are considerate, as well. I can just barely hear them talking and laughing in the distance. The frogs croaking along the lake's edge are much louder. All the same, I have company.

Four days of deep woods solitude. Not bad considering that I've been camped in this shelter the entire time. But it's a different situation now. I have neighbors. There are people only fifty yards away. The spell has been broken. Suddenly I'm thinking about cutting this outing short. When Todd and Phil head out tomorrow, I'll be alone again but for how long?

Tomorrow is Friday. The weekend begins. Surely other hikers will come along tomorrow evening. I didn't come out here to socialize. What the hell, I've had my time alone here. Five days is good enough. Six isn't necessary.

Past midnight, I can still hear Todd and Phil in the distance. I crack a smile. In a strange way, it's nice to have company. It's not their fault that I'm still awake. Have to stop thinking, I tell myself, and get back to sleep. Five days or six, it doesn't matter – not right now, anyway. I'll make a decision about that in the morning.

Daybreak. I awaken to croaking frogs and a host of songbirds: wood thrush, veery, white-throated sparrow, blue jay, nuthatch and, of course, the not-so-common loon. Mosquitoes whine at the net. A sparrow chips loudly as it hops across camp. And just now something unseen is splashing out of the water. A brook trout perhaps?

It's a pleasant morning with a faint breeze stirring the lake's surface, a mist clinging to the trees on Noisey Ridge, and a few sunlit clouds loitering in the east. Another perfect summer day is unfolding. I feel blessed just to be here. That much said, I make an important decision before crawling out of bed: I'm headed out today.

I've done what I set out to do when I came here. I have stayed put, grooved on the wild, and let the thoughts flow. I have a notebook full of ruminations. When a butterfly lands on your knee as you're pondering the relationships between God, humankind and nature, well, that's pretty hard to beat. Time to move on. There's no point hanging around here just to socialize. So I'm headed out today. I'll take my sweet time breaking camp, but I'll be back on the trail before noon. Looking forward to it, actually.

After changing into clean clothes, I fix breakfast. I have enough water to drink and clean up this morning so I don't need to disturb my sleeping neighbors right away. The camp stove hisses loudly. Matika wolfs down her breakfast then sniffs around, creeping slowly away from the shelter. She wants to go visit Todd and Phil. I make her stay close by.

Dueling loons. Once again, one calls from the open water right in front of the shelter while the other answers from the far end of the lake. Their songs echo through the hills. I've been hearing the call of loons for days yet it still enthralls me. How could anyone spend a little time with loons and not fall in love with the wild?

While enjoying my last few hours at Pillsbury Lake, I feel the presence of the sacred. It's something I've felt many times before. In fact, I feel it every time I spend a day or two in a wild place. I have felt it in Alaska, the Maine woods, the Cascades, the Rockies, the White Mountains, on my home turf the Green Mountains, and many times here in the Adirondacks. All wild places are sacred places. That becomes apparent after a while. But that doesn't mean one has to be religious to appreciate them. As Diane Ackerman wrote in her book, *Deep Play*: "What is sacred goes far beyond the religious." One can be an atheist and still feel the presence of the sacred in a place like this. The sacred is that which cuts right to the core of our being, what opens us to the world at large. The sacred is what we feel whenever we make a strong connection to nature. The sacred is the beauty and wonder of the world, and a sudden awareness of being completely immersed in it. I experience this every time I go deep into the forest. Is there any better reason to come out here?

Todd and Phil are up. I can hear them puttering about their camp. I need water. It's time to go socialize. Matika is eager to do so.

13

I greet Todd and Phil while making my way down to the lake's edge to pump water. They are on the move, simultaneously breaking camp and fixing breakfast. In the time it takes me to fill two liter bottles, they have their tent down and a good portion of their gear packed up. Matika goes straight to Phil for snugs and gets them. She has a way of finding dog lovers. Todd and Phil are headed to West Lake today. That's not far away. At the rate they're moving right now, they could be on the trail within an hour and to West Lake by early afternoon. I invite them to join me for a mid-morning campfire before they head out. They say they will.

Back at the shelter I putter about, taking down the mosquito net, clothesline, and slowly packing up my gear. There's an armload of sticks next to the fire pit ready to go. I build a small tipi of kindling over some birch bark and wait for my guests. I make a final journal entry then glass the lake with my binoculars one last time, looking for the loons. I collect a small bag of trash to carry out – stuff left behind by other backpackers. Still no guests. What's taking them so long? Maybe they've changed their mind. I ignite the tipi and start feeding sticks into it. Wind gusts make the fire burn hot and fast. By the time Todd and Phil appear, my small pile of wood is burnt up and the campfire is down to embers. I'm embarrassed. They sit down along the edge of the shelter, pans of food in hand, and converse with me anyway.

They aren't as young as they looked by lamplight last night. Middle-aged, I'd say, which is still young to me. Todd is a big bear of a man and quite outgoing. Phil is slender and mild mannered. They hail from a small town just outside Ithaca. Todd is an experienced backpacker. Phil has done a lot of canoe camping. Todd pulls out a map then asks me a few questions about West Lake. A decade has passed since my stay at West Lake so I couch all my answers with "last time I was there." They're especially interested in finding a good place to land just off the Northville-Placid Trail. Like me, they want to avoid other people.

Shortly after they finish eating, Todd and Phil say goodbye. A few minutes later, I hear them chatting quietly while making their way back to French Louie Trail. Then Matika and I are on our own again. Just like that.

Late morning. My gear is gathered on the shelter floor, all nice and tidy. The ashes in the fire pit are cold. There's nothing left to do here. I take one last look around then pack up and go.

The trail is much easier to walk now than it was five days ago. Matika and I have some difficulty negotiating a small bog without getting wet and muddy, otherwise the ground underfoot is solid for the most part. There are a few other mud holes along the way, yes, but they're easy to bypass. Sunlight filters through the trees, illuminating the understory. I cut my pace in order to fully savor the brilliant green vegetation all around me. After two miles of forest daydreaming, I reach the well-marked junction with the main trail. Down goes my pack and out comes a water bottle. Matika and I empty it.

Two young women come along while I'm taking a break. They're going only as far as Sampson Lake today but hope to do the 23-mile loop to West Lake, Cedar Lakes and back during the next three days. I tell them a couple fellows who stayed with me at Pillsbury Lake last night are several hours ahead of them.

From the trail junction, a wide, well-beaten path eases gradually downhill towards the trailhead. Only two miles left. I stop halfway down the slope in an effort to delay my inevitable exit from the woods. It's a beautiful summer day with ideal temps and a light breeze. I look around, admiring the forest canopy, thinking how lucky I am to be out here grooving on the wild. In my 60s now yet still enjoying these solitary jaunts into deep woods. Most people my age no longer have the time, the inclination, or the physical ability to do so. Either that or they've forgotten how rewarding a deep forest walk can be. One of my old hiking buddies has already passed away. I feel very lucky to be here.

A bit farther down the trail, I encounter a thirty-something couple hiking hard and fast uphill. "How far are you going?" I ask.

"South Lake," the young woman says.

"Oh yeah, I went there once. Long ago."

"Is it nice?"

"Yeah, it's nice there," I respond, "It's – It's all beautiful." And where am I coming from? I pause for a moment before telling the couple that I've been camped at Pillsbury Lake the past five days, alone for the most part – just me and my dog. I really don't want to get into what I did or didn't do there.

"That sounds fantastic!" the woman exclaims, beaming a great big smile.

"Yes, it was…lovely," I say for lack of a better word, turning away so they don't see the tears welling in my eyes. Then I finish my hike.

While signing out of the trailhead register, I notice that half a dozen groups have entered the woods since yesterday, and nearly all of them are doing the 23-mile loop. And there's still plenty of time for more groups to show up. Had I stayed one more night at the Pillsbury Lake Shelter, I would have had company for sure. Looking around, I count a dozen vehicles in the parking lot, including a pick-up that belongs to a forest ranger. A pile of wood is neatly stacked nearby – the remnants of that downed tree I cut away five days ago. That makes me smile.

The drive out of the woods is long and dusty with no big puddles to traverse. With her head out the window, Matika enjoys all the passing sights and smells. I do the math in my head, estimating that I'll be home by 6 o'clock. I'll have to text Judy about that on my fancy timepiece – as soon as service is available. Won't she be surprised to see me a day early. But I got everything I wanted out of this excursion and then some. Now all I have to do is go home and make sense of all the blather scribbled into my field journal. That's a tall order, indeed.

About the Author

Walt McLaughlin received a degree in philosophy from Ohio University in 1977 and has been wondering, wandering and writing ever since. He has over a dozen books in print, including a narrative about his immersion in the Alaskan bush, *Arguing with the Wind*, and one about backpacking through the Adirondacks, *The Allure of Deep Woods*. He is also the force behind a small press called Wood Thrush Books, and has selected and published the works of several 19th Century writers including *The Laws of Nature: Excerpts from the Writings of Ralph Waldo Emerson*. He lives in Swanton, Vermont with his wife, Judy.

For more information about Walt's books, visit the WTB website: **www.woodthrushbooks.com**

Go to **www.facebook.com\WaltMcLaughlin** to check out his Facebook page, or read his regularly posted blogs at **www.woodswanderer.com**